American Negro Poetry

AMERICAN NEGRO POETRY

REVISED EDITION

EDITED AND WITH AN INTRODUCTION

BY *Arna Bontemps*

WITH UPDATED BIOGRAPHICAL NOTES

HILL AND WANG

A division of Farrar, Straus and Giroux

New York

Hill and Wang
A division of Farrar, Straus and Giroux
19 Union Square West, New York 10003

Library of Congress catalog card number: 72-95044
ISBN-13: 978-0-8090-1564-1
ISBN-10: 0-8090-1564-1

www.fsgbooks.com

26   28   30   32   34   33   31   29   27

A Note from the Publishers

In 1963, Arna Bontemps first edited this outstanding selection of poems by African Americans. Bontemps's achievement was to bring together great voices of the twentieth century—writers as diverse as Countee Cullen, Langston Hughes, Ted Joans, Audre Lorde, and Richard Wright—and to show the development of their poetic tradition. Bontemps was in a perfect position to accomplish this, for he had served for many years as librarian of Fisk University and had worked on several other poetry anthologies, most notably *The Poetry of the Negro: 1746–1949*, which he co-edited with his good friend Langston Hughes. His many books include *Anyplace But Here*, *The Story of the Negro* (a runner-up for the Newbery Award), *100 Years of Negro Freedom*, and *The Harlem Renaissance Remembered*. In 1974, Bontemps revised this anthology to include the poems of many postwar black writers, including Audre Lorde, Nikki Giovanni, and Bob Kaufman, among others. This new edition, issued by the publishers in 1996, reprints the poems of Bontemps's revised anthology with updated biographical notes.

Contents

Frank Lamont Phillips

Marvin Wyche, Jr.

Introduction

THE POETRY OF the American Negro sometimes seems hard to pin down. Like his music, from spirituals and gospel songs to blues, jazz, and bebop, it is likely to be marked by a certain special riff, an extra glide, a kick where none is expected, and a beat for which there is no notation. It follows the literary traditions of the language it uses, but it does not hold them sacred. As a result, there has been a tendency for critics to put it in a category by itself, outside the main body of American poetry.

But Negroes take to poetry as they do to music. In the Harlem Renaissance of the twenties poetry led the way for the other arts. It touched off the awakening that brought novelists, painters, sculptors, dancers, dramatists, and scholars of many kinds to the notice of a nation that had nearly forgotten about the gifts of its Negro people. And almost the first utterance of the revival struck an arresting new note:

> I've known rivers ancient as the world and older
> than the flow of human blood in human veins.

Soon thereafter the same generation responded to a poem that had been written even earlier and which Claude McKay included in his *Harlem Shadows*, 1922. "So much have I forgotten in ten years," the first stanza began. It closed with

> I have forgotten much, but still remember
> The poinsettia's red, blood-red in warm December.

And before these notes subsided, Jean Toomer raised his voice:

> Pour O pour that parting soul in song,
> O pour it in the sawdust glow of night. . . .
> And let the valley carry it along.

The Renaissance was on, and it was richly quotable, with Helene Johnson saying:

> Ah little road, brown as my race is brown,
> Dust of the dust, they must not bruise you down.

And Countee Cullen:

> I doubt not God is good, well-meaning, kind,
> And did He stoop to quibble could tell why
> The little buried mole continues blind,
> Why flesh that mirrors Him must some day die. . . .
> Yet do I marvel at this curious thing:
> To make a poet black, and bid him sing!

And Frank Horne:

> I buried you deeper last night
> You with your tears and your tangled hair.

And Donald Jeffrey Hayes:

> No rock along the road but knows
> The inquisition of his toes;
> No journey's end but what can say:
> He paused and rested here a day!

And Waring Cuney:

> She does not know
> Her beauty,
> She thinks her brown body
> Has no glory.

In those days a good many of the New York group went to "The Dark Tower" on 136th Street, a sort of club room maintained for them by one of their fans, to weep because they felt an injustice in the critics' insistence upon calling them *Negro* poets instead of poets. This attitude was particularly displeasing to Countee Cullen. But a few of his associates were not sure this was bad. Three decades later, considering the isolation of so many contemporary poets (including some Negroes) and their private language—well, they were still wondering. But it can be fairly said that most Negro poets in the United States remain near enough to their folk origins to prefer a certain simplicity of expression.

The poets of the Harlem Renaissance were born nearly two hundred years after Lucy Terry, the semiliterate slave girl, wrote "Bars Fight," a verse account of an Indian raid on old Deerfield in 1746. Phillis Wheatley, whose *Poems on Various Subjects, Religious and Moral* attracted much favorable attention in 1773, was born in Senegal, West Africa, sold into slavery in early childhood, and brought to Boston in 1761. "A Poem by Phillis, A Negro Girl in Boston, on the Death of the

Reverend George Whitefield," published when she was just seventeen, heralded the beginning of a unique writing career. When her health failed and she was advised by doctors to take an ocean voyage, Phillis embarked for England. In London the delicate girl was a success, and there her collection of verse was first issued.

Lucy Terry and Phillis Wheatley, along with such other American Negroes as Jupiter Hammon and George Moses Horton, belong to a tradition of writers in bondage which goes back to Aesop and Terence. There is no clear indication that Aesop succeeded in writing himself out of servitude. Nor did Lucy Terry, so far as is known, nor George Moses Horton of North Carolina, though Horton did manage to survive till the Northern armies set him free. But Terence and Phillis Wheatley both won their freedom by their writing.

Paul Laurence Dunbar, a son of former slaves, appeared about 120 years after Phillis and greeted the twentieth century with several volumes of lyrics, including such representative poems as "Dawn," "The Party," "We Wear the Mask," and "Compensation," together with scores of others which, more than half a century later, have a host of admirers to whom they remain fresh and poignant. His *Complete Poems*, 1913, is still in print.

A strong sense of melody and rhythm was a feature of Dunbar's poetry, as it has been of nearly all the Negro poets of the United States. Dunbar's delightful country folk, his broad, often humorous, dialect failed to create a tradition, however. Later Negro poets have held that the effective use of dialect in poetry is limited to humor and pathos. Accordingly, most of them have abandoned it.

A contemporary of Dunbar's was James Weldon Johnson, but Johnson's *God's Trombones*, 1927, a collection of folk sermons in verse and his most important poetic achievement, was not completed till the Harlem awakening. But meanwhile William Stanley Braithwaite, best known for his series of annual *Anthologies of Magazine Verse*, 1913 to 1929, published two volumes of his own lyrics, 1904 and 1908, neither of them recognizable in any way as "Negro poetry." Selected editions of Johnson's and Braithwaite's poems were published in 1930 and 1948 respectively.

Angelina W. Grimké, Anne Spencer, and Georgia Douglas Johnson are women whose poems appeared here and there before the Harlem poets arrived. Miss Grimké's "The Black Finger," Miss Spencer's "Letter to My Sister," and Miss Johnson's "The Heart of a Woman" are typical. Fenton Johnson, their contemporary, is remembered best for free verse vignettes. Three small volumes of his poetry came out between 1914 and 1916.

With the arrival of Claude McKay in the United States Negro poetry welcomed its strongest voice since Dunbar. Born in Jamaica, British West Indies, McKay published his first book, *Songs of Jamaica*, at the age of nineteen. *Constab Ballads,* written in West Indian dialect, followed about a year later, and presently the young McKay migrated to the United States to attend Tuskegee Institute and later Kansas State University as a student of agriculture. Two years of this was enough for him. He moved on to New York and began contributing verse to American magazines. McKay went to Europe in 1919 and published in London his slight but appealing collection *Spring in New Hampshire,* 1920. On returning to America he became associated with Max Eastman in the editing of the *Liberator. Harlem Shadows,* the book by which he became widely known to poetry lovers, and which touched off much subsequent literary activity in Harlem, came out in 1922. "The Tropics in New York" and the famous sonnet "If We Must Die" represent McKay's range as well as his special quality. Attention was drawn to the universality of the latter when Winston Churchill quoted it as the conclusion to his address before the joint houses of Congress prior to the entrance of the United States into World War II. The Prime Minister did not name the author, but in this context McKay's powerful lines gave the embattled allies an emotional jolt as Churchill read:

> If we must die, O let us nobly die,
> So that our precious blood may not be shed
> In vain; then even the monsters we defy
> Shall be constrained to honor us though dead!
>
> . . .
>
> Like men we'll face the murderous, cowardly pack,
> Pressed to the wall, dying, but fighting back!

The poems of Langston Hughes, meanwhile, had been appearing in the *Crisis,* a magazine which had since 1911 welcomed contributions by Negro poets. But Hughes quickly identified himself as a distinct new voice. "The Negro Speaks of Rivers" appeared soon after his graduation from high school in 1920 and was widely reprinted. The first collection of his poems was *The Weary Blues,* 1926, but many volumes have followed, all of them marked by an ease of expression and a naturalness of feeling that make them seem almost as if they had never been composed at all. Hughes's art can be likened to that of Jelly Roll Morton and the other creators of jazz. His sources are street music. His language is Harlemese. In his way he too is an American original.

Countee Cullen, another of the poets who helped to create the mood of the twenties in Negro poetry, was quite different. Educated in New York City, he adopted the standard models, from John Keats to E. A. Robinson. But the ideas that went into Cullen's sonnets and quatrains were new in American poetry. His long poem "Color," which gave its title to his first book, 1925, published while Cullen was still an undergraduate at New York University, is the poet's wrestling with the problem of race prejudice as he saw and experienced it. His "Heritage" shows him seeking a nostalgic link with the Africa of his forebears. Both are included, along with the other poems by which he wished to be remembered, in his *On These I Stand*, 1947. Cullen was sometimes published in the *Crisis* in his early days but more often in *Opportunity: Journal of Negro Life*. Both of these outlets were important to the development of Negro writers in the twenties, but Cullen was more successful than most of the group in getting his poems into the general magazines in the United States.

Jean Toomer's small output belongs to this same period. His *Cane*, 1924, like Sterling Brown's *Southern Road* a decade later, highlighted significant folk values.

Several Negro poets have received critical attention since the Harlem period. Margaret Walker won the Yale University Younger Poets award in 1942 with her volume *For My People*, the title poem of which has become a favorite of Negro speakers and readers. Her "Molly Means" has become popular with verse choirs. Gwendolyn Brooks's first book was *A Street in Bronzeville*, 1945. Her *Annie Allen*, which followed in 1949, was awarded the Pulitzer Prize for poetry, the first time this honor had been given to any Negro writer. She has since published fiction as well as poetry for children. Owen Dodson's *Powerful Long Ladder*, 1946, seems, despite the implication of the title, to draw more from the New Poetry of our time than from Negro sources. The books of Melvin B. Tolson's poetry also represent two attitudes toward his material. *Rendezvous with America*, 1944, shows the influence of Langston Hughes and Negro folklore. His *Libretto for the Republic of Liberia*, 1953, while treating a Negro theme, is a surprisingly sophisticated exercise in New poetics. Nevertheless, it won him honors from the government of Liberia.

Two questions are likely to occur to the reader introduced for the first time to the poetry of the American Negro. What happened after the death of Phillis Wheatley to the impulse represented by her poetry? What explanation is there, in other words, for the seeming silence of slave poets between the publication of her book and Paul Laurence Dunbar's first? The answer is simple enough, once the history of the period is recalled.

Legal restrictions on the education of slaves were introduced after Phillis Wheatley's time. The purpose, of course, was to keep from the slave news and propaganda likely to incite a lust for freedom. During the era of the French Revolution and the Haitian Insurrections this was regarded as a serious matter, and slave uprisings, or attempted uprisings, in Virginia, South Carolina, and elsewhere in the United States added to the anxiety. Penalities were imposed on people who violated the restrictions. This explains the stratagems devised by alert slave boys like Frederick Douglass of Maryland, as described in his autobiography, to acquaint themselves with the rudiments of written communication. The cunning device employed by Richard Wright for drawing books from the Memphis Public Library in his boyhood was a similar effort in the present century.

Denied even the A B C's, slave poetry had no choice but to go underground. Self-expression was obliged to become oral. Whether or not this was a blessing in disguise is a matter of opinion. Nevertheless, the suppression of book learning by slaves appears to have coincided with the earliest musical expression in the form now known as Negro spirituals. The survival of "Roll, Jordan, Roll," for example, among slaves from the United States isolated on a Carribean island since 1824, would seem to place the beginnings of these songs very early in the nineteenth century, if not indeed in the eighteenth, allowing for the time it usually took such songs to develop and become generally known. Thus the elegies, commemorations, and devotional poems of Phillis Wheatley, in the spirit of John Calvin and the manner of her English and American literary contemporaries, were replaced as poetry by the lyrics of "Swing Low, Sweet Chariot," "Deep River," "My Lord What a Morning," and "O Mary, What You Gonna Name That Pretty Little Baby." James Weldon Johnson pays his respects to this creativity in his poem "O Black and Unknown Bards."

Some contemporary black poets are still moved by the bittersweet cadences with which Dunbar greeted this century. Many are still turned on by the unction with which Hughes and Cullen awakened the lilting twenties. Others, from Bob Kaufman to Nikki Giovanni to Marvin Wyche and Frank Lamont Phillips, reflect more recent influences. Negro experience in America has found a vastly satisfying medium of expression in music. If occasionally this has been felt as a mood of our time, in the broad sense, perhaps that is another matter. The lyrics of the spirituals are certainly as vital and valid as the music, and the same can be said of blues and of ballads like "John Henry." From these sources comes a kind of poetic tradition and American Negro poets have frequently associated themselves with it. However, it is well to remember that Phillis Wheatley wrote with some success before it existed, and there is certainly no way to predict what spirit will move the newest Negro poet.

ARNA BONTEMPS

American Negro Poetry

O Black and Unknown Bards / JAMES WELDON JOHNSON

O black and unknown bards of long ago,
How came your lips to touch the sacred fire?
How, in your darkness, did you come to know
The power and beauty of the minstrel's lyre?
Who first from midst his bonds lifted his eyes?
Who first from out the still watch, lone and long,
Feeling the ancient faith of prophets rise
Within his dark-kept soul, burst into song?

Heart of what slave poured out such melody
As "Steal away to Jesus"? On its strains
His spirit must have nightly floated free,
Though still about his hands he felt his chains.
Who heard great "Jordan roll"? Whose starward eye
Saw chariot "swing low"? And who was he
That breathed that comforting, melodic sigh,
"Nobody knows de trouble I see"?

What merely living clod, what captive thing,
Could up toward God through all its darkness grope,
And find within its deadened heart to sing
These songs of sorrow, love and faith, and hope?
How did it catch that subtle undertone,
That note in music heard not with the ears?
How sound the elusive reed so seldom blown,
Which stirs the soul or melts the heart to tears.

Not that great German master in his dream
Of harmonies that thundered amongst the stars
At the creation, ever heard a theme
Nobler than "Go down, Moses." Mark its bars

How like a mighty trumpet-call they stir
The blood. Such are the notes that men have sung
Going to valorous deeds; such tones there were
That helped make history when Time was young.

There is a wide, wide wonder in it all,
That from degraded rest and servile toil
The fiery spirit of the seer should call
These simple children of the sun and soil.
O black slave singers, gone, forgot, unfamed,
You—you alone, of all the long, long line
Of those who've sung untaught, unknown, unnamed,
Have stretched out upward, seeking the divine.

You sang not deeds of heroes or of kings;
No chant of bloody war, no exulting paean
Of arms-won triumphs; but your humble strings
You touched in chord with music empyrean.
You sang far better than you knew; the songs
That for your listeners' hungry hearts sufficed
Still live,—but more than this to you belongs:
You sang a race from wood and stone to Christ.

Go Down Death (A Funeral Sermon)
JAMES WELDON JOHNSON

Weep not, weep not,
She is not dead;
She's resting in the bosom of Jesus.
Heart-broken husband—weep no more;
Grief-stricken son—weep no more;
She's only just gone home.

Day before yesterday morning,
God was looking down from his great, high heaven,
Looking down on all his children,
And his eye fell on Sister Caroline,
Tossing on her bed of pain.
And God's big heart was touched with pity,
With the everlasting pity.

And God sat back on his throne,
And he commanded that tall, bright angel standing at his
      right hand:
Call me Death!
And that tall, bright angel cried in a voice
That broke like a clap of thunder:
Call Death!—Call Death!
And the echo sounded down the streets of heaven
Till it reached away back to that shadowy place,
Where Death waits with his pale, white horses.

And Death heard the summons,
And he leaped on his fastest horse,
Pale as a sheet in the moonlight.
Up the golden street Death galloped,
And the hoof of his horse struck fire from the gold,
But they didn't make no sound.
Up Death rode to the Great White Throne,
And waited for God's command.

And God said: Go down, Death, go down,
Go down to Savannah, Georgia,
Down in Yamacraw,
And find Sister Caroline.
She's borne the burden and heat of the day,
She's labored long in my vineyard,
And she's tired—
She's weary—
Go down, Death, and bring her to me.

And Death didn't say a word,
But he loosed the reins on his pale, white horse,

And he clamped the spurs to his bloodless sides,
And out and down he rode,
Through heaven's pearly gates,
Past suns and moons and stars;
On Death rode,
And the foam from his horse was like a comet in the sky;
On Death rode,
Leaving the lightning's flash behind;
Straight on down he came.

While we were watching round her bed,
She turned her eyes and looked away,
She saw what we couldn't see;
She saw Old Death. She saw Old Death.
Coming like a falling star.
But Death didn't frighten Sister Caroline;
He looked to her like a welcome friend.
And she whispered to us: I'm going home,
And she smiled and closed her eyes.

And Death took her up like a baby,
And she lay in his icy arms,
But she didn't feel no chill.
And Death began to ride again—
Up beyond the evening star,
Out beyond the morning star,
Into the glittering light of glory,
On to the Great White Throne.
And there he laid Sister Caroline
On the loving breast of Jesus.

And Jesus took his own hand and wiped away her tears,
And he smoothed the furrows from her face,
And the angels sang a little song,
And Jesus rocked her in his arms,
And kept a-saying: Take your rest,
Take your rest, take your rest.
Weep not—weep not,
She is not dead;
She's resting in the bosom of Jesus.

Dawn / PAUL LAURENCE DUNBAR

An angel, robed in spotless white,
Bent down and kissed the sleeping Night.
Night woke to blush; the sprite was gone.
Men saw the blush and called it Dawn.

Compensation / PAUL LAURENCE DUNBAR

Because I had loved so deeply,
    Because I had loved so long,
God in His great compassion
    Gave me the gift of song.

Because I have loved so vainly,
    And sung with such faltering breath,
The Master, in infinite mercy,
    Offers the boon of death.

The Debt / PAUL LAURENCE DUNBAR

This is the debt I pay
Just for one riotous day,
Years of regret and grief,
Sorrow without relief.

Pay it I will to the end—
Until the grave, my friend,
Gives me a true release—
Gives me the clasp of peace.

Slight was the thing I bought,
Small was the debt I thought,
Poor was the loan at best—
God! but the interest!

Life / PAUL LAURENCE DUNBAR

A crust of bread and a corner to sleep in,
A minute to smile and an hour to weep in,
A pint of joy to a peck of trouble,
And never a laugh but the moans come double:
      And that is life!

A crust and a corner that love makes precious,
With the smile to warm and the tears to refresh us:
And joy seems sweeter when cares come after,
And a moan is the finest of foils for laughter:
      And that is life!

My Sort o' Man / PAUL LAURENCE DUNBAR

I don't believe in ristercrats
   An' never did, you see;

The plain ol' homelike sorter folks
  Is good enough fur me.
O' course, I don't desire a man
  To be too tarnal rough,
But then I think all folks should know
  When they air nice enough.

Now, there is folks in this here world,
  From peasant up to king,
Who want to be so awful nice
  They overdo the thing.
That's jest the thing that makes me sick,
  An' quicker than a wink
I set it down that them same folks
  Ain't half so good's you think.

I like to see a man dress nice,
  In clothes becomin', too;
I like to see a woman fix
  As women orter do;
An' boys an' gals I like to see
  Look fresh an' young an' spry.—
We all must have our vanity
  An' pride before we die.

But I jedge no man by his clothes,--
  Nor gentleman nor tramp;
The man that wears the finest suit
  May be the biggest scamp,
An' he whose limbs are clad in rags
  That make a mournful sight,
In life's great battle may have proved
  A hero in the fight.

I don't believe in 'ristercrats;
  I like the honest tan
That lies upon the healthful cheek
  An' speaks the honest man;
I like to grasp the brawny hand
  That labor's lips have kissed,

7

For he who has not labored here
   Life's greatest pride has missed,—

The pride to feel that yo'r own strength
   Has cleaved fur you the way
To heights to which you were not born,
   But struggled day by day.
What though the thousands sneer an' scoff,
   An' scorn yo'r humble birth?
Kings are but subject; you are king
   By right o' royal worth.

The man who simply sits an' waits
   Fur good to come along,
Ain't worth the breath that one would take
   To tell him he is wrong.
Fur good ain't flowin' round this world
   Fur ev'ry fool to sup;
You've got to put yo'r see-ers on,
   An' go an' hunt it up.

Good goes with honesty, I say,
   To honor an' to bless;
To rich an' poor alike it brings
   A wealth o' happiness.
The 'ristercrats ain't got it all,
   Fur much to their su'prise,
That's one of earth's most blessed things
   They can't monopolize.

The Party / PAUL LAURENCE DUNBAR

Dey had a gread big pahty down to Tom's de othah night;
Was I dah? You bet! I nevah in my life see sich a sight;

8

All de folks f'om fou' plantations was invited, an' dey come,
Dey come troopin' thick ez chillun when dey hyeahs a fife
an' drum.
Evahbody dressed deir fines'— Heish yo' mouf an' git away,
Ain't seen sich fancy dressin' sence las' quah'tly meetin'
day;
Gals all dressed in silks an' satins, not a wrinkle ner a crease,
Eyes a-battin', teeth a-shinin', haih breshed back ez slick ez
grease;
Sku'ts all tucked an' puffed an' ruffled, evah blessed seam an'
stitch;
Ef you'd seen 'em wif deir mistus, couldn't swahed to which
was which.
Men all dressed up in Prince Alberts, swallertails 'u'd tek you'
bref!
I cain't tell you nothin' 'bout it, yo' ought to seen it fu' yo'se'f.
Who was dah? Now who you askin'? How you 'spect I gwine
to know?
You mus' think I stood an' counted evahbody at de do'.
Ole man Babah's house boy Isaac, brung dat gal,
Malindy Jane,
Huh a-hangin' to his elbow, him a struttin' wif a cane;
'My, but Hahvey Jones was jealous! seemed to stick him lak
a tho'n;
But he laughed with Viney Cahteh, tryin' ha'd to not let on,
But a pusson would'a' noticed f'om de d'rection of his look,
Dat he was watchin' ev'ry step dat Ike an' Lindy took.
Ike he foun' a cheer an' asked huh: "Won't you set down?" wif
a smile,
An' she answe'd up a-bowin', "Oh, I reckon 'tain't wuth while."
Dat was jes' fu' style, I reckon, 'cause she sot down jes' de
same,
An' she stayed dah 'twell he fetched huh fu' to jine some so't
o' game;
Den I hyeahd huh sayin' propah, ez she riz to go away,
"Oh, you raly mus' excuse me, fu' I hardly keers to play."
But I seen huh in a minute wif de othahs on de flo',
An' dah wasn't any one o' dem a-playin' any mo';

Comin' down de flo' a-bowin' an' a-swayin' an' a-swingin',
Puttin' on huh high-toned mannahs all de time dat she was
    singin':
"Oh, swing Johnny up an' down, swing him all aroun',
Swing Johnny up an' down, swing him all aroun',
Oh, swing Johnny up an' down, swing him all aroun',
Fa' yu well, my dahlin'."
Had to laff at ole man Johnson, he's a caution now you bet—
Hittin' clost onto a hunderd, but he's spry an' nimble yet;
He 'lowed how a-so't o' gigglin', "I ain't ole, I'll let you see,
D'ain't no use in gettin' feeble, now you youngstahs jes' watch
    me,"
An' he grabbed ole Aunt Marier—weighs th'ee hundred mo'er
    less,
An' he spun huh 'roun' de cabin swingin' Johnny lak de res'.
Evahbody laffed an' hollahed: "Go it, swing huh, Uncle Jim!"
An' he swing huh too, I reckon, lak a youngstah, who but him.
Dat was bettah'n young Scott Thomas, tryin' to be so awful
    smaht.
You know when dey gits to singin' an' dey comes to dat ere
    paht:
            "In some lady's new brick house,
        In some lady's gyahden.
            Ef you don't let me out, I will jump out,
        So fa' you well, my dahlin'."
Den dey's got a circle 'roun' you, an' you's got to break de
    line;
Well, dat dahky was so anxious, lak to bust hisse'f a-tryin';
Kep' on blund'rin' 'round' an' foolin' 'twell he giv' one great
    big jump,
Broke de line, an' lit head-fo'most in de fiahplace right plump;
Hit 'ad fiah in it, mind you; well, I thought my soul I'd bust,
Tried my best to keep f'om laffin' but hit seemed like die I
    must!
Y' ought to seen dat man a-scramblin' f'om de ashes an' de
    grime.
Did it bu'n him! Sich a question, why he didn't give it time;

Th'ow'd dem ashes and dem cindahs evah which-a-way I
  guess,
An' you nevah did, I reckon, clap yo' eyes on sich a mess;
Fu' he sholy made a picter an' a funny one to boot,
Wif his clothes all full o' ashes an' his face all full o' soot.
Well, hit laked to stopped de pahty, an' I reckon lak ez not
Dat it would ef Tom's wife, Mandy, hadn't happened on de
  spot,
To invite us out to suppah—well, we scrambled to de table,
An' I'd lak to tell you 'bout it—what we had—but I ain't able,
Mention jes' a few things, dough I know I hadn't orter,
Fu' I know 'twill staht a hank'rin' an' yo' mouf'll mence to
  worter.
We had wheat bread white ez cotton an' a egg pone jes' like
  gol',
Hog jole, bilin' hot an' steamin', roasted shoat, an' ham sliced
  cold—
Look out! What's de mattah wif you? Don't be fallin' on de
  flo';
Ef it's go'n to 'fect you dat way, I won't tell you nothin' mo'.
Dah now—well, we had hot chittlin's—now you's tryin' ag'in
  to fall,
Cain't you stan' to hyeah about it? S'pose you'd been an' seed
  it all;
Seed dem gread big sweet pertaters, layin' by de possum's
  side,
Seed dat coon in all his gravy, reckon den you'd up and died!
Mandy 'lowed "you all mus' 'scuse me, d' wa'n't much upon
  my she'ves,
But I's done my bes' to suit you, so set down an' he'p
  yo'se'ves."
Tom, he 'lowed: "I don't b'lieve in 'pologizin' an' perfessin',
Let 'em tek it lak dey ketch it. Eldah Thompson, ask de
  blessin'."
Wish you'd seed dat colo'ed preachah cleah his th'oat an' bow
  his head;
One eye shet an' one eye open,—dis is evah wud he said:

11

"Lawd, look down in tendah mussy on sich generous hea'ts
ez dese;
Makes us truly thankful, amen. Pass dat possum, ef you
please."
Well, we eat and drunk ouah po'tion, 'twell dah wasn't
nothin' lef',
An' we felt jes' like new sausage, we was mos' nigh stuffed
to def!
Tom, he knowed how we'd be feelin', so he had de fiddlah
'roun',
An' he made us cleah de cabin fu' to dance dat suppah down.
Jim, de fiddlah, chuned his fiddle, put some rosum on his
bow,
Set a pine box on de table, mounted it an' let huh go!
He's a fiddlah, now I tell you, an' he made dat fiddle ring,
'Twell de ol'est an' de lamest had to give deir feet a fling.
Jigs, cotillions, reels an' break-downs, cordrills an' a waltz er
two;
Bless yo' soul, dat music winged 'em an' dem people lak to
flew.
Cripple Joe, de ole rheumatic, danced dat flo' f'om side to
middle,
Th'owed away his crutch an' hopped it, what's rheumatics
'ginst a fiddle?
Eldah Thompson got so tickled dat he lak to lo' his grace,
Had to tek bofe feet an' hol' dem so's to keep 'em in deir
place.
An' de Christuns an' de sinnahs got so mixed up on dat flo',
Dat I don't see how dey'd pahted ef de trump had chanced
to blow.
Well, we danced dat way an' capahed in de mos' redic'lous
way,
'Twell de roostahs in de bahnyard cleahed deir th'oats an'
crowed fu' day.
Y' ought to been dah, fu' I tell you evahthing was rich an'
prime,
An' dey ain't no use in talkin', we jes' had one scrumptious
time!

12

A Song / PAUL LAURENCE DUNBAR

Thou art the soul of a summer's day,
Thou art the breath of the rose.
   But the summer is fled
   And the rose is dead.
Where are they gone, who knows, who knows?

Thou art the blood of my heart o' hearts,
Thou art my soul's repose,
   But my heart grows numb
   And my soul is dumb.
Where art thou, love, who knows, who knows?

Thou art the hope of my after years—
Sun for my winter snows.
   But the years go by
   'Neath a clouded sky.
Where shall we meet, who knows, who knows?

Sympathy / PAUL LAURENCE DUNBAR

I know what the caged bird feels, alas!
When the sun is bright on the upland slopes;
When the wind stirs soft through the springing grass
And the river flows like a stream of glass;
When the first bird sings and the first bud opes,
And the faint perfume from its chalice steals—
I know what the caged bird feels!

I know why the caged bird beats his wing
Till its blood is red on the cruel bars;

For he must fly back to his perch and cling
When he fain would be on the bough a-swing;
And a pain still throbs in the old, old scars
And they pulse again with a keener sting—
I know why he beats his wing!

I know why the caged bird sings, ah me,
When his wing is bruised and his bosom sore,
When he beats his bars and would be free;
It is not a carol of joy or glee,
But a prayer that he sends from his heart's deep core,
But a plea, that upward to Heaven he flings—
I know why the caged bird sings!

We Wear the Mask / PAUL LAURENCE DUNBAR

We wear the mask that grins and lies,
It hides our cheeks and shades our eyes,—
This debt we pay to human guile;
With torn and bleeding hearts we smile,
And mouth with myriad subtleties.

Why should the world be overwise,
In counting all our tears and sighs?
Nay, let them only see us, while
    We wear the mask.

We smile, but, O great Christ, our cries
To Thee from tortured souls arise.
We sing, but oh, the clay is vile
Beneath our feet, and long the mile;
But let the world dream otherwise,
    We wear the mask.

14

Rhapsody / WILLIAM STANLEY BRAITHWAITE

I am glad daylong for the gift of song,
For time and change and sorrow;
For the sunset wings and the world-end things
Which hang on the edge of tomorrow.
I am glad for my heart whose gates apart
Are the entrance-place of wonders,
Where dreams come in from the rush and din
Like sheep from the rains and thunders.

Scintilla / WILLIAM STANLEY BRAITHWAITE

I kissed a kiss in youth
    Upon a dead man's brow;
And that was long ago—
    And I'm a grown man now.

It's lain there in the dust,
    Thirty years and more—
My lips that set a light
    At a dead man's door.

To Clarissa Scott Delany / ANGELINE W. GRIMKE

She has not found herself a hard pillow
    And a long hard bed,

A chilling cypress, a wan willow
  For her gay young head . . .
    These are for the dead.

Does the violet-lidded twilight die
  And the piercing dawn
And the white clear moon and the night-blue sky . . .

Does the shimmering note
In the shy, shy throat
Of the swaying bird?

O, does children's laughter
Live not after
It is heard?

Does the dear, dear shine upon dear, dear things,
In the eyes, on the hair,
On waters, on wings . . .
Live no more anywhere?

Does the tang of the sea, the breath of frail flowers,
  Of fern crushed, of clover,
Of grasses at dark, of the earth after showers
  Not linger, not hover?

Does the beryl in tarns, the soft orchid in haze,
The primrose through treetops, the unclouded jade
Of the north sky, all earth's flamings and russets and grays
  Simply smudge out and fade?

And all loveliness, all sweetness, all grace,
All the gay questing, all wonder, all dreaming,
They that cup beauty that veiled opaled vase,
Are they only the soul of a seeming?

O, hasn't she found just a little, thin door
And passed through and closed it between?
O, aren't those her light feet upon that light floor,
  . . . That her laughter? . . . O, doesn't she lean
As we do to listen? . . . O, doesn't it mean
  She is only unseen, unseen?

The Black Finger / ANGELINA W. GRIMKÉ

I have just seen a beautiful thing
    Slim and still,
Against a gold, gold sky,
    A straight cypress,
    Sensitive,
    Exquisite,
A black finger
Pointing upwards.
Why, beautiful, still finger are you black?
And why are you pointing upwards?

For Jim, Easter Eve / ANNE SPENCER

If ever a garden was a Gethsemane,
with old tombs set high against
the crumpled olive tree—and lichen,
this, my garden, has been to me.
For such as I none other is so sweet:
Lacking old tombs, here stands my grief,
and certainly its ancient tree.

Peace is here and in every season
a quiet beauty.
The sky falling about me
evenly to the compass . . .
What is sorrow but tenderness now
in this earth-close frame of land and sky
falling constantly into horizons
of east and west, north and south;
what is pain but happiness here

amid these green and wordless patterns,—
indefinite texture of blade and leaf:

Beauty of an old, old tree,
last comfort in Gethsemane.

Lines to a Nasturtium (A lover muses) / ANNE SPENCER

Flame-flower, Day-torch, Mauna Loa,
I saw a daring bee, today, pause, and soar,
        Into your flaming heart;
Then did I hear crisp crinkled laughter
As the furies after tore him apart?
        A bird, next, small and humming,
Looked into your startled depths and fled . . .
Surely, some dread sight, and dafter
        Than human eyes as mine can see,
Set the stricken air waves drumming
        In his flight.

Day-torch, Flame-flower, cool-hot Beauty,
I cannot see, I cannot hear your fluty
Voice lure your loving swain,
But I know one other to whom you are in beauty
Born in vain;
Hair like the setting sun,
Her eyes a rising star,
Motions gracious as reeds by Babylon, bar
All your competing;
Hands like, how like, brown lilies sweet,
 Cloth of gold were fair enough to touch her feet . . .
Ah, how the senses flood at my repeating,
As once in her fire-lit heart I felt the furies
Beating, beating.

Letter to My Sister / ANNE SPENCER

It is dangerous for a woman to defy the gods;
To taunt them with the tongue's thin tip,
Or strut in the weakness of mere humanity,
Or draw a line daring them to cross;
The gods who own the searing lightning,
The drowning waters, the tormenting fears,
The anger of red sins . . .
Oh, but worse still if you mince along timidly—
Dodge this way or that, or kneel, or pray,
Or be kind, or sweat agony drops,
Or lay your quick body over your feeble young,
If you have beauty or plainnness, if celibate,
Or vowed—the gods are Juggernaut,
Passing over each of us . . .
    Or this you may do:
Lock your heart, then quietly,
And, lest they peer within,
Light no lamp when dark comes down.
Raise no shade for sun,
Breathless must your breath come thru,
If you'd die and dare deny
The gods their godlike fun!

Morning Light the Dew-Drier / EFFIE LEE NEWSOME

In Africa little black boys, "human brooms," are sent before the explorers into jungle grasses that tower many feet to tread down a path and meet sometimes the lurking leopard or hyena. They are called Dew-driers.

Brother to the firefly—
For as the firefly lights the night,
So lights he the morning—
Bathed in the dank dews as he goes forth
Through heavy menace and mystery
Of half-waking tropic dawn,
Behold a little black boy,
A naked black boy,
Sweeping aside with his slight frame
Night's pregnant tears,
And making a morning path to the light
For the tropic traveler!

Bathed in the blood of battle,
Treading toward a new morning,
May not his race, its body long bared
To the world's disdain, its face schooled to smile
For a light to come,
May not his race, even as the dew-boy leads,
Light onward men's minds toward a time
When tolerance, forbearance
Such as reigned in the heart of One
Whose heart was gold,
Shall shape the earth for that fresh dawning
After the dews of blood?

Common Dust / GEORGIA DOUGLAS JOHNSON

And who shall separate the dust
Which later we shall be:
Whose keen discerning eye will scan
And solve the mystery?

20

The high, the low, the rich, the poor,
The black, the white, the red,
And all the chromatique between,
Of whom shall it be said:

Here lies the dust of Africa;
Here are the sons of Rome;
Here lies one unlabelled
The world at large his home!

Can one then separate the dust,
Will mankind lie apart,
When life has settled back again
The same as from the start?

Trifle / GEORGIA DOUGLAS JOHNSON

Against the day of sorrow
Lay by some trifling thing
A smile, a kiss, a flower
For sweet remembering.

Then when the day is darkest
Without one rift of blue
Take out your little trifle
And dream your dream anew.

The Poet Speaks / GEORGIA DOUGLAS JOHNSON

How much living have you done?
From it the patterns that you weave
Are imaged:
Your own life is your totem pole,
Your yard of cloth,
Your living.

How much loving have you done?
How full and free your giving?
For living is but loving
And loving only giving.

I Want to Die While You
Love Me / GEORGIA DOUGLAS JOHNSON

I want to die while you love me,
While yet you hold me fair,
While laughter lies upon my lips
And lights are in my hair.

I want to die while you love me.
I could not bear to see,
The glory of this perfect day,
Grow dim—or cease to be.

I want to die while you love me.
Oh! who would care to live
Till love has nothing more to ask,
And nothing more to give.

I want to die while you love me,
And bear to that still bed
Your kisses, turbulent, unspent,
To warm me when I'm dead.

Your World / GEORGIA DOUGLAS JOHNSON

Your world is as big as you make it.
I know, for I used to abide
In the narrowest nest in a corner,
My wings pressing close to my side.

But I sighted the distant horizon
Where the sky line encircled the sea
And I throbbed with a burning desire
To travel this immensity.

I battered the cordons around me
And cradled my wings on the breeze
Then soared to the uttermost reaches
With rapture, with power, with ease!

Lovelight / GEORGIA DOUGLAS JOHNSON

Strange atoms we unto ourselves
Soaring a strange demesne
With life and death the darkened doors
And love the light between.

Prejudice / GEORGIA DOUGLAS JOHNSON

These fell miasmic rings of mist,
   with ghoulish menace bound,
Like noose-horizons tightening my
   little world around.
They still the soaring will to wing,
   to dance, to speed away.
And fling the soul insurgent back
   into its shell of clay.
Beneath incrusted silences, a seeth-
   ing Etna lies,
The fire of whose furnaces may
   sleep, but never dies!

Conquest / GEORGIA DOUGLAS JOHNSON

My pathway lies through worse than death;
I meet the hours with bated breath.
My red blood boils, my pulses thrill,
I live life running up a hill.

Ah, no, I need no paltry play
Of make-shift tilts for holiday:
For I was born against the tide
And I must conquer that denied.

I shun no hardship, fear no foe;
The future calls and I must go:
I charge the line and dare the spheres
As I go fighting down the years.

The Daily Grind / FENTON JOHNSON

If Nature says to you,
"I intend you for something fine,
For something to sing the song
That only my whirling stars can sing,
For something to burn in the firmament
With all the fervor of my golden sun,
For something to moisten the parched souls
As only my rivulets can moisten the parched,"

What can you do?

If the System says to you,
"I intend you to grind and grind
Grains of corn beneath millstones;
I intend you to shovel and sweat
Before a furnace of Babylon;
I intend you for grist and meat
To fatten my pompous gods
As they wallow in an alcoholic nectar,"

What can you do?

Naught can you do
But watch that eternal battle
Between Nature and the System.
You cannot blame God,
You cannot blame man;
For God did not make the System,
Neither did man fashion Nature.
You can only die each morning,
And live again in the dreams of the night.
If Nature forgets you,
If the System forgets you,
God has blest you.

The World Is a Mighty Ogre / FENTON JOHNSON

I could love her with a love so warm
You could not break it with a fairy charm;
I could love her with a love so bold
It would not die, e'en tho' the world grew cold.

I cannot cross the bridge, nor climb the tower,—
I cannot break the spell of magic power;
The rules of man forbid me raise my sword—
Have mercy on a humble bard, O Lord!

A Negro Peddler's Song / FENTON JOHNSON

*(The pattern of this song was sung by a Negro peddler in a
Chicago alley.)*

Good Lady,
I have corn and beets,
Onions, too, and leeks,
And also sweet potat-y.

Good Lady,
Buy for May and John;
And when work is done
Give a bite to Sadie.

Good Lady,
I have corn and beets,
Onions, too, and leeks,
And also sweet potat-y.

The Old Repair Man / FENTON JOHNSON

God is the Old Repair Man.
When we are junk in Nature's storehouse he takes us apart.
What is good he lays aside; he might use it some day.
What has decayed he buries in six feet of sod to nurture
     the weeds.
Those we leave behind moisten the sod with their tears;
But their eyes are blind as to where he has placed
     the good.
Some day the Old Repair Man
Will take the good from its secret place
And with his gentle, strong hands will mold
A more enduring work—a work that will defy Nature—
And we will laugh at the old days, the troubled days,
When we were but a crude piece of craftsmanship,
When we were but an experiment in Nature's laboratory. . . .
It is good we have the Old Repair Man.

Counting / FENTON JOHNSON

Go count the stars!
Whirling worlds of light,
Endless balls of fire,
Lonely Evening Star,
Dancing Morning Star,
Silvery necklaces in a jewel box of mist
For the wedding of an angel to an earth-daughter.
Pray, is there one who can count the stars?

Go count the unborn souls!
Many are the cherubs at Michael's Gate.

Awaiting their chubby bodies and a mother's arms.
So in their day flitted Caesars, Napoleons,
Alexanders whilst cherub Miltons chanted,
"We are Michael's angels, sweet Michael's angels."
Pray, is there one who can count the unborn souls?

The Tropics in New York / CLAUDE McKAY

Bananas ripe and green, and gingerroot,
    Cocoa in pods and alligator pears,
And tangerines and mangoes and grapefruit,
    Fit for the highest prize at parish fairs,

Set in the window, bringing memories
    Of fruit trees laden by low-singing rills,
And dewy dawns, and mystical blue skies
    In benediction over nunlike hills.

My eyes grew dim, and I could no more gaze;
    A wave of longing through my body swept,
And, hungry for the old, familiar ways,
    I turned aside and bowed my head and wept.

Outcast / CLAUDE McKAY

For the dim regions whence my fathers came
My spirit, bondaged by the body, longs.

28

Words felt, but never heard, my lips would frame;
My soul would sing forgotten jungle songs.
I would go back to darkness and to peace,
But the great western world holds me in fee,
And I may never hope for full release
While to its alien gods I bend my knee.
Something in me is lost, forever lost,
Some vital thing has gone out of my heart,
And I must walk the way of life a ghost
Among the sons of earth, a thing apart.

For I was born, far from my native clime,
Under the white man's menace, out of time.

St. Isaac's Church, Petrograd / Claude McKay

Bow down my soul in worship very low
And in the holy silences be lost.
Bow down before the marble Man of Woe,
Bow down before the singing angel host.
What jewelled glory fills my spirit's eye,
What golden grandeur moves the depths of me!
The soaring arches lift me up on high,
Taking my breath with their rare symmetry.

Bow down my soul and let the wondrous light
Of beauty bathe thee from her lofty throne,
Bow down before the wonder of man's might.
Bow down in worship, humble and alone,
Bow lowly down before the sacred sight
Of man's Divinity alive in stone.

Flame-Heart / CLAUDE McKAY

So much have I forgotten in ten years,
  So much in ten brief years! I have forgot
What time the purple apples come to juice,
  And what month brings the shy forget-me-not.
I have forgot the special, startling season
  Of the pimento's flowering and fruiting;
What time of year the ground doves brown the fields
  And fill the noonday with their curious fluting.
I have forgotten much, but still remember
The poinsettia's red, blood-red in warm December.

I still recall the honey-fever grass,
  But cannot recollect the high days when
We rooted them out of the ping-wing path
  To stop the mad bees in the rabbit pen.
I often try to think in what sweet month
  The languid painted ladies used to dapple
The yellow byroad mazing from the main,
  Sweet with the golden threads of the rose apple.
I have forgotten—strange—but quite remember
The poinsettia's red, blood-red in warm December.

What weeks, what months, what time of the mild year
  We cheated school to have our fling at tops?
What days our wine-thrilled bodies pulsed with joy
  Feasting upon blackberries in the copse?
Oh, some I know! I have embalmed the days,
  Even the sacred moments when we played,
All innocent of passion, uncorrupt,
  At noon and evening in the flame-heart's shade.
We were so happy, happy, I remember,
Beneath the poinsettia's red in warm December.

If We Must Die / Claude McKay

If we must die—let it not be like hogs
Hunted and penned in an inglorious spot,
While round us bark the mad and hungry dogs,
Making their mock at our accursed lot.
If we must die—oh, let us nobly die,
So that our precious blood may not be shed
In vain; then even the monsters we defy
Shall be constrained to honor us though dead!
Oh, Kinsmen! We must meet the common foe;
Though far outnumbered, let us show us brave,
And for their thousand blows deal one deathblow!
What though before us lies the open grave?
Like men we'll face the murderous, cowardly pack,
Pressed to the wall, dying, but fighting back!

The White House / Claude McKay

Your door is shut against my tightened face,
And I am sharp as steel with discontent;
But I possess the courage and the grace
To bear my anger proudly and unbent.
The pavement slabs burn loose beneath my feet,
A chafing savage, down the decent street;
And passion rends my vitals as I pass,
Where boldly shines your shuttered door of glass.
Oh, I must search for wisdom every hour,
Deep in my wrathful bosom sore and raw,
And find in it the superhuman power
To hold me to the letter of your law!

Oh, I must keep my heart inviolate
Against the potent poison of your hate.

Georgia Dusk / JEAN TOOMER

The sky, lazily disdaining to pursue
   The setting sun, too indolent to hold
   A lengthened tournament for flashing gold,
Passively darkens for night's barbecue,

A feast of moon and men and barking hounds,
   An orgy for some genius of the South
   With blood-hot eyes and cane-lipped scented mouth,
Surprised in making folk songs from soul-sounds.

The sawmill blows its whistle, buzz saws stop,
   And silence breaks the bud of knoll and hill,
   Soft settling pollen where plowed lands fulfill
Their early promise of a bumper crop.

Smoke from the pyramidal sawdust pile
   Curls up, blue ghosts of trees, tarrying low
   Where only chips and stumps are left to show
The solid proof of former domicile.

Meanwhile, the men, with vestiges of pomp,
   Race memories of king and caravan,
   High priests, an ostrich, and a juju-man,
Go singing through the footpaths of the swamp.

Their voices rise . . . the pine trees are guitars,
   Strumming, pine needles fall like sheets of rain . . .
   Their voices rise . . . the chorus of the cane
Is caroling a vesper to the stars . . .

O singers, resinous and soft your songs
   Above the sacred whisper of the pines,
   Give virgin lips to cornfield concubines,
Bring dreams of Christ to dusky cane-lipped throngs.

Song of the Son / JEAN TOOMER

Pour O pour that parting soul in song,
O pour it in the sawdust glow of night,
Into the velvet pine-smoke air tonight,
And let the valley carry it along.
And let the valley carry it along.

O land and soil, red soil and sweet-gum tree,
So scant of grass, so profligate of pines,
Now just before an epoch's sun declines
Thy son, in time, I have returned to thee,
Thy son, I have, in time, returned to thee.

In time, for though the sun is setting on
A song-lit race of slaves, it has not set;
Though late, O soil, it is not too late yet
To catch thy plaintive soul, leaving, soon gone,
Leaving, to catch thy plaintive soul soon gone.

O Negro slaves, dark purple ripened plums,
Squeezed, and bursting in the pine-wood air,
Passing, before they strip the old tree bare
One plum was saved for me, one seed becomes

An everlasting song, a singing tree,
Caroling softly souls of slavery,
What they were, and what they are to me,
Caroling softly souls of slavery.

Brown River, Smile / Jean Toomer

It is a new America,
To be spiritualized by each new American.

Lift, lift, thou waking forces!
Let us feel the energy of animals,
The energy of rumps and bull-bent heads
Crashing the barrier to man.
It must spiral on!
A million million men, or twelve men,
Must crash the barrier to the next higher form.

Beyond plants are animals,
Beyond animals is man,
Beyond man is the universe.

The Big Light,
Let the Big Light in!

O thou, Radiant Incorporeal,
The I of earth and of mankind, hurl
Down these seaboards, across this continent,
The thousand-rayed discus of thy mind,
And above our walking limbs unfurl
Spirit-torsos of exquisite strength!

The Mississippi, sister of the Ganges,
Main artery of earth in the western world,
Is waiting to become
In the spirit of America, a sacred river.
Whoever lifts the Mississippi
Lifts himself and all America;
Whoever lifts himself
Makes that great brown river smile.
The blood of earth and the blood of man
Course swifter and rejoice when we spiritualize.

The old gods, led by an inverted Christ,
A shaved Moses, a blanched Lemur,

And a moulting thunderbird,
Withdrew into the distance and soon died,
Their dust and seed falling down
To fertilize the five regions of America.

We are waiting for a new God.

The old peoples—
The great European races sent wave after wave
That washed the forests, the earth's rich loam,
Grew towns with the seeds of giant cities,
Made roads, laid golden rails,
Sang once of its swift achievement,
And died congested in machinery.
They say that near the end
It was a world of crying men and hard women,
A city of goddam and Jehovah
Baptized in industry
Without benefit of saints,
Of dear defectives
Winnowing their likenesses from weathered rock
Sold by national organizations of undertakers.

Someone said:
    Suffering is impossible
    On cement sidewalks, in skyscrapers,
    In motorcars;
    Steel cannot suffer—
    We die unconsciously
    Because possessed by a nonhuman symbol.

Another cried:
    It is because of thee, O Life,
    That the first prayer ends in the last curse.

Another sang:
    Late minstrels of the restless earth,
    No muteness can be granted thee,
    Lift thy laughing energies
    To that white point which is a star.

The great African races sent a single wave
And singing riplets to sorrow in red fields,
Sing a swan song, to break rocks
And immortalize a hiding water boy.

> I'm leaving the shining ground, brothers,
> I sing because I ache,
> I go because I must,
> Brothers, I am leaving the shining ground;
> Don't ask me where,
> I'll meet you there,
> I'm leaving the shining ground.

The great red race was here.
In a land of flaming earth and torrent-rains,
Of red sea-plains and majestic mesas,
At sunset from a purple hill
The Gods came down;
They serpentined into pueblo,
And a white-robed priest
Danced with them five days and nights;
But pueblo, priest, and Shalicos
Sank into the sacred earth
To fertilize the five regions of America.

> Hi-ye, hi-yo, hi-yo
> Hi-ye, hi-yo, hi-yo,
> A lone eagle feather,
> An untamed Navaho,
> The ghosts of buffaloes,
> Hi-ye, hi-yo, hi-yo,
> Hi-ye, hi-yo, hi-yo.

We are waiting for a new people.

O thou, Radiant Incorporeal,
The I of earth and of mankind, hurl
Down these seaboards, across this continent,
The thousand-rayed discus of thy mind,
And above our walking limbs unfurl
Spirit-torsos of exquisite strength!

The east coast is masculine,
The west coast is feminine,
The middle region is the child—
Forces of reconciling
And generator of symbols.

> Thou, great fields, waving thy growths across
>   the world,
> Couldest thou find the seed which started thee?
> Can you remember the first great hand to sow?
> Have you memory of His intention?
> Great plains, and thou, mountains,
> And thou, stately trees, and thou,
> America, sleeping and producing with the seasons,
> No clever dealer can divide,
> No machine can undermine thee.

The prairie's sweep is flat infinity,
The city's rise is perpendicular to farthest star,
I stand where the two directions intersect,
At Michigan Avenue and Walton Place,
Parallel to my countrymen,
Right-angled to the universe.

It is a new America,
To be spiritualized by each new American.

Dark Symphony / Melvin B. Tolson

I   ALLEGRO MODERATO

Black Crispus Attucks taught
        Us how to die
Before white Patrick Henry's bugle breath

Uttered the vertical
            Transmitting cry:
"Yea, give me liberty, or give me death."

And from that day to this
            Men black and strong
For Justice and Democracy have stood,
Steeled in the faith that Right
            Will conquer Wrong
And Time will usher in one brotherhood.

No Banquo's ghost can rise
            Against us now
And say we crushed men with a tyrant's boot
Or pressed the crown of thorns
            On Labor's brow,
Or ravaged lands and carted off the loot.

II   LENTO GRAVE

The centuries-old pathos in our voices
Saddens the great white world,
And the wizardry of our dusky rhythms
Conjures up shadow-shapes of ante-bellum years:

Black slaves singing *One More River to Cross*
In the torture tombs of slave ships,
Black slaves singing *Steal Away to Jesus*
In jungle swamps,
Black slaves singing *The Crucifixion*
In slave pens at midnight,
Black slaves singing *Swing Low, Sweet Chariot*
In cabins of death,
Black slaves singing *Go Down, Moses*
In the canebrakes of the Southern Pharaohs.

III   ANDANTE SOSTENUTO

They tell us to forget
The Golgotha we tread . . .
We who are scourged with hate,

38

A price upon our head.
They who have shackled us
Require of us a song,
They who have wasted us
Bid us o'erlook the wrong.

They tell us to forget
Democracy is spurned.
They tell us to forget
The Bill of Rights is burned.
Three hundred years we slaved,
We slave and suffer yet:
Though flesh and bone rebel,
They tell us to forget!

Oh, how can we forget
Our human rights denied?
Oh, how can we forget
Our manhood crucified?
When Justice is profaned
And plea with curse is met,
When Freedom's gates are barred,
Oh, how can we forget?

IV TEMPO PRIMO

The New Negro strides upon the continent
In seven league boots . . .
The New Negro
Who sprang from the vigor-stout loins
Of Nat Turner, gallows-martyr for Freedom,
Of Joseph Cinquez, Black Moses of the Amistad Mutiny,
Of Frederick Douglass, oracle of the Catholic Man,
Of Sojourner Truth, eye and ear of Lincoln's legions,
Of Harriet Tubman, St. Bernard of the Underground
          Railroad.

None in the Land can say
To us black men Today:
You send the tractors on their bloody path,
And create Oakies for *The Grapes of Wrath*.
You breed the slum that breeds a *Native Son*
To damn the good earth Pilgrim Fathers won.

None in the Land can say
To us black men Today:
You dupe the poor with rags-to-riches tales,
And leave the workers empty dinner pails.
You stuff the ballot box, and honest men
Are muzzled by your demogogic din.

None in the Land can say
To us black men Today:
You smash stock markets with your coined blitzkriegs
And make a hundred million guinea pigs.
You counterfeit our Christianity,
And bring contempt upon Democracy.

None in the Land can say
To us black men Today:
You prowl when citizens are fast asleep,
And hatch Fifth Column plots to blast the deep
Foundations of the State and leave the Land
A vast Sahara with a Fascist brand.

None in the Land can say
To us black men Today:
You send flame-gutting tanks, like swarms of flies,
And plump a hell from dynamiting skies.
You fill machine-gunned towns with rotting dead—
A No Man's Land where children cry for bread.

VI   TEMPO DI MARCIA

Out of abysses of Illiteracy,
Through labyrinths of Lies,

Across wastelands of Disease . . .
We advance!

Out of dead-ends of Poverty,
Through wildernesses of Superstition,
Across barricades of Jim Crowism . . .
We advance!

With the Peoples of the World . . .
We advance!

Kid Stuff / FRANK HORNE

DECEMBER, 1942

The wise guys
tell me
that Christmas
is Kid Stuff . . .
Maybe they've got
something there—
Two thousand years ago
three wise guys
chased a star
across a continent
to bring
frankincense and myrrh
to a Kid
born in a manger
with an idea in his head . . .

And as the bombs
crash
all over the world
today

the real wise guys
know
that we've all
got to go chasing stars
again
in the hope
that we can get back
some of that
Kid Stuff
born two thousand years ago.

Notes Found Near a Suicide / FRANK HORNE

TO ALL OF YOU

My little stone
Sinks quickly
Into the bosom of this deep, dark pool
Of oblivion . . .
I have troubled its breast but little
Yet those far shores
That knew me not
Will feel the fleeting, furtive kiss
Of my tiny concentric ripples . . .

TO MOTHER

I came
In the blinding sweep
Of ecstatic pain,
I go
In the throbbing pulse
Of aching space—

In the eons between
I piled upon you
Pain on pain
Ache on ache
And yet as I go
I shall know
That you will grieve
And want me back . . .

TO CATALINA

Love thy piano, Oh girl,
It will give you back
Note for note
The harmonies of your soul.
It will sing back to you
The high songs of your heart.
It will give
As well as take . . .

TO TELIE

You have made my voice
A rippling laugh
But my heart
A crying thing . . .
'Tis better thus:
A fleeting kiss
And then,
The dark . . .

TO "CHICK"

Oh Achilles of the moleskins
And the gridiron
Do not wonder
Nor doubt that this is I
That lies so calmly here—
This is the same exultant beast
That so joyously

Ran the ball with you
In those far-flung days of abandon.
You remember how recklessly
We revelled in the heat and the dust
And the swirl of conflict?
You remember they called us
The Terrible Two?
And you remember
After we had battered our heads
And our bodies
Against the stonewall of their defense,—
You remember the signal I would call
And how you would look at me
In faith and admiration
And say "Let's go," . . .
How the lines would clash
And strain,
And how I would slip through
Fighting and squirming
Over the line
To victory.
You remember, Chick? . . .
When you gaze at me here
Let that same light
Of faith and admiration
Shine in your eyes
For I have battered the stark stonewall
Before me . . .
I have kept faith with you
And now
I have called my signal,
Found my opening
And slipped through
Fighting and squirming
Over the line
To victory. . . .

TO WANDA

To you, so far away
So cold and aloof,
To you, who knew me so well,
This is my last Grand Gesture
This is my last Great Effect
And as I go winging
Through the black doors of eternity
Is that thin sound I hear
Your applause? . . .

TO JAMES

Do you remember
How you won
That last race . . . ?
How you flung your body
At the start . . .
How your spikes
Ripped the cinders
In the stretch . . .
How you catapulted
Through the tape . . .
Do you remember . . . ?
Don't you think
I lurched with you
Out of those starting holes . . . ?
Don't you think
My sinews tightened
At those first
Few strides . . .
And when you flew into the stretch
Was not all my thrill
Of a thousand races
In your blood . . . ?
At your final drive
Through the finish line
Did not my shout

Tell of the
Triumphant ecstasy
Of victory . . . ?
Live
As I have taught you
To run, Boy—
It's a short dash
Dig your starting holes
Deep and firm
Lurch out of them
Into the straightaway
With all the power
That is in you
Look straight ahead
To the finish line
Think only of the goal
Run straight
Run high
Run hard
Save nothing
And finish
With an ecstatic burst
That carries you
Hurtling
Through the tape
To victory . . .

TO THE POETS:

Why do poets
Like to die
And sing raptures to the grave?

They seem to think
That bitter dirt
Turns sweet between the teeth.

I have lived
And yelled hosannas
At the climbing stars

I have lived
And drunk deep
The deceptive wine of life . . .

And now, tipsy and reeling
From its dregs
I die . . .

Oh, let the poets sing
Raptures to the grave.

TO HENRY:

I do not know
How I shall look
When I lie down here
But I really should be smiling
Mischievously . . .
You and I have studied
Together
The knowledge of the ages
And lived the life of Science
Matching discovery for discovery—
And yet
In a trice
With a small explosion
Of this little machine
In my hand
I shall know
All
That Aristotle, Newton, Lavoisier, and Galileo
Could not determine
In their entire
Lifetimes . . .
And the joke of it is,
Henry,
That I have
Beat you to it . . .

TO ONE WHO CALLED ME "NIGGER":

You are Power
And send steel ships hurtling
From shore to shore . . .

You are Vision
And cast your sight through eons of space
From world to world . . .

You are Brain
And throw your voice endlessly
From ear to ear . . .

You are Soul
And falter at the yawning chasm
From White to Black . . .

TO CAROLINE:

Your piano
Is the better instrument . . .
Yesterday
Your fingers
So precisely
Touched the cold keys—
A nice string
Of orderly sounds
A proper melody . . .
Tonight
Your hands
So wantonly
Caressed my tingling skin—
A mad whirl
Of cacophony,
A wild chanting . . .
Your piano
Is the better instrument.

TO ALFRED:

I have grown tired of you
And your wife
Sitting there
With your children,
Little bits of you
Running about your feet
And you two so calm
And cold together . . .
It is really better
To lie here
Insensate
Than to see new life
Creep upon you
Calm and cold
Sitting there . . .

TO YOU:

All my life
They have told me
That You
Would save my Soul
That only
By kneeling in Your House
And eating of Your Body
And drinking of Your Blood
Could I be born again . . .
And yet
One night
In the tall black shadow
Of a windy pine
I offered up
The Sacrifice of Body
Upon the altar
Of her breast . . .
You
Who were conceived

49

Without ecstasy
Or pain
Can you understand
That I knelt last night
In Your House
And ate of Your Body
And drank of Your Blood.
. . . and thought only of her?

To a Persistent Phantom / FRANK HORNE

I buried you deeper last night
You with your tears
And your tangled hair
You with your lips
That kissed so fair
I buried you deeper last night.

I buried you deeper last night
With fuller breasts
And stronger arms
With softer lips
And newer charms
I buried you deeper last night.

Deeper . . . ay, deeper
And again tonight
Till that gay spirit
That once was you
Will tear its soul
In climbing through . . .
Deeper . . . ay, deeper
I buried you deeper last night.

Symphony / FRANK HORNE

Is this dancing sunlight
prancing through the windows
of this limping room
mocking us
who strain
and stagger
with legs strapped in leather
and braced
with cold steel
or tottering
on crutch
or cane . . . ?

Is this carnival of light
mocking
the ponderous rhythms
and stumbling pace
and the tears
and gasps of supplication
to make quick
the sickened limb . . . ?

Does it taunt
or does it beckon
with warm affection
and hope . . . ?

Are prancing light
and faltering crutch
variations of the dance
of suns
and moons
and pain
and glory
point and counterpoint
to the baton

of the maestro
to whom
all rhythms
and periods
are the stuff
of the symphony
of life?

McDonogh Day in New Orleans / MARCUS B. CHRISTIAN

The cotton blouse you wear, your mother said,
After a day of toil, "I guess I'll buy it";
For ribbons on your head and blouse she paid
Two-bits a yard—as if you would deny it!

And nights, after a day of kitchen toil,
She stitched your re-made skirt of serge—once blue—
Weary of eye, beneath a lamp of oil:
McDonogh would be proud of her and you.

Next, came white "creepers" and white stockings, too—
They almost asked her blood when they were sold;
Like some dark princess, to the school go you,
With blue larkspur and yellow marigold;
But few would know—or even guess this fact:
How dear comes beauty when a skin is black.

Dialect Quatrain / Marcus B. Christian

This ain't Torquemada—
'Tain't no "Scourge o'God"—
Hit's jess li'l ole New Awleens's
"Makeum-Tell-It Squad."

Sister Lou / Sterling A. Brown

Honey
When de man
Calls out de las' train
You're gonna ride,
Tell him howdy.

Gather up yo' basket
An' yo' knittin' an' yo' things,
An' go on up an' visit
Wid frien' Jesus fo' a spell.

Show Marfa
How to make yo' greengrape jellies,
An' give po' Lazarus
A passel of them Golden Biscuits.

Scald some meal
Fo' some rightdown good spoonbread
Fo' li'l box-plunkin' David.

An' sit aroun'
An' tell them Hebrew Chillen
All yo' stories. . . .

Honey
Don't be feared of them pearly gates,
Don't go 'round to de back,
No mo' dataway
Not evah no mo'.

Let Michael tote yo' burden
An' yo' pocketbook an' evah thing
'Cept yo' Bible,
While Gabriel blows somp'n
Solemn but loudsome
On dat horn of his'n.

Honey
Go Straight on to de Big House,
An' speak to yo' God
Widout no fear an' tremblin'.

Then sit down
An' pass de time of day awhile.

Give a good talkin' to
To yo' favorite 'postle Peter,
An' rub the po' head
Of mixed-up Judas,
An' joke awhile wid Jonah.

Then, when you gits de chance,
Always rememberin' yo' raisin',
Let 'em know youse tired
Jest a mite tired.

Jesus will find yo' bed fo' you
Won't no servant evah bother wid yo' room.
Jesus will lead you
To a room wid windows
Openin' on cherry trees an' plum trees
Bloomin' everlastin'.

An' dat will be yours
Fo' keeps.

Den take yo' time. . . .
Honey, take yo' bressed time.

When de Saints Go Ma'chin' Home
STERLING A. BROWN

I

He'd play, after the bawdy songs and blues,
After the weary plaints
Of "Trouble, Trouble deep down in muh soul,"
Always one song in which he'd lose the role
Of entertainer to the boys. He'd say
"My mother's favorite." And we knew
That what was coming was his chant of saints
"When de Saints go ma'chin' home . . ."
And that would end his concert for the day.

Carefully as an old maid over needlework,
Or, as some black deacon, over his Bible, lovingly,
He'd tune up specially for this. There'd be
No chatter now, no patting of the feet.
After a few slow chords, knelling and sweet
Oh, when de saints go ma'chin' home
Oh, when de sayaints goa ma'chin' home . . .
He would forget
The quieted bunch, his dimming cigarette
Stuck into a splintered edge of the guitar.
Sorrow deep hidden in his voice, a far
And soft light in his strange brown eyes;
Alone with his masterchords, his memories . . .
    Lawd, I wanna be one in nummer
    When de saints go ma'chin' home.

Deep the bass would rumble while the treble scattered
     high
For all the world like heavy feet a trompin' toward the sky.
With shrill-voiced women getting 'happy'
All to celestial tunes.
The chap's few speeches helped me understand
The reason why he gazed so fixedly
Upon the burnished strings.
For he would see
A gorgeous procession to 'de Beulah Land'
Of Saints—his friends—'a climbin' fo' deir wings.'
Oh, when de saints go ma'chin' home
Lawd, I wanna be one o' dat nummer
When de saints goa ma'chin' home . . .

          II

There'd be—so ran his dream—
"Old Deacon Zachary
With de asthmy in his chest
A puffin' an' a wheezin'
Up de golden stair
Wid de badges of his lodges
Strung acrost his heavin' breast
An' de hoggrease jest shinin'
In his coal-black hair . . .

An' old Sis Joe
In huh big straw hat
An' huh wrapper flappin'
Flappin' in de heavenly win'
An' huh thin-soled easy walkers
Goin' pitty pitty pat
Lawd, she'd have to ease her corns
When she got in!"
Oh, when de saints go ma'chin' home.
"Ole Elder Peter Johnson
Wid his corncob jes a puffin'
And de smoke a rollin'

Like storm clouds out behin'
Crossin' de cloud mountains
Widout slowin' up fo' nuffin'
Steamin' up de grade
Lak Wes' bound No. 9.
An' de little brown-skinned chillen
Wid deir skinny legs a dancin'
Jes' a kickin' up ridic'lous
To de heavenly band
Lookin' at de Great Drum Major
On a white hoss jes' a prancin'
Wid a gold and silver drumstick
A waggin' in his han'.
Oh when de sun refuse to shine
Oh when de mo-on goes down
        In Blood . . .

"Old Maumee Annie
Wid huh washin' done
An' huh las' piece o' laundry
In de renchin' tub,
A wavin' sof' pink han's
To de much obligin' sun
An' her feet a moverin' now
To a swif' rub-a-dub;
And old Grampa Eli
Wid his wrinkled old haid
A puzzlin' over summut
He ain' understood
Intendin' to ask Peter
Pervidin' he hain't skyaid
Jes' what mought be de meanin'
        Of de moon in blood? . . .
When de saints go ma'chin' home . . ."

        III

Whuffolks, he dreams, will have to stay outside
Being so onery. But what is he to do

With that red brakeman who once let him ride
An empty, going home? Or with that kindfaced man
Who paid his songs with board and drink and bed?
Or with the Yankee Cap'n who left a leg
At Vicksburg? *Mought be a place, he said*
Mought be another mansion for white saints
A smaller one than hisn . . . not so gran'
As for the rest . . . oh, let them howl and beg.
Hell would be good enough, if big enough
Widout no shade trees, lawd, widout no rain
Whuffolks sho to bring nigger out behin'
Excep'—when de saints go ma'chin' home.

IV

Sportin' Legs would not be there—nor lucky Sam
Nor Smitty, nor Hambone, nor Hardrock Gene
An' not too many guzzlin', cuttin' shines,
Nor bootleggers to keep his pockets clean.
An' Sophie wid de sof' smile on her face,
Her foolin' voice, her strappin' body, brown
Lak coffee doused wid milk—she had been good
To him, wid lovin', money, and wid food.—
But saints and heaven didn't seem to fit
Jes rite wid Sophy's beauty—nary bit—
She mought stir trouble, somehow, in dat peaceful place
Mought be some dressed up dudes in dat fair town.

V

Ise got a dear ole modder
She is in hebben I know . . .
He sees
Mammy
L'il mammy—wrinkled face
Her brown eyes, quick to tears—to joy
With such happy pride in her
Guitar plunkin' boy.
Oh, kain't I be one in nummer?

Mammy
With deep religion defeating the grief
Life piled so closely about her
Ise so glad trouble doan las' alway' . . .
And her dogged belief
That some fine day
She'd go a ma'chin'
When de saints go ma'chin' home.
He sees her ma'chin' home, ma'chin' along,
Her perky joy shining in her furrowed face,
Her weak and quavering voice singing her song—
The best chair set apart for her worn-out body
In that restful place . . .
    I pray to de Lawd I'll meet her
    When de saints go ma'chin' home.

VI

He'd shuffle off from us, always, at that,—
His face a brown study beneath his torn brimmed hat.
His broad shoulders slouching, his old box strung
Around his neck;—he'd go where we
Never could follow him—to Sophie probably,
Or to his dances in old Tinbridge flat.

Solace / CLARISSA SCOTT DELANY

My window opens out into the trees
And in that small space
Of branches and of sky
I see the seasons pass
Behold the tender green
 Give way to darker heavier leaves.

The glory of the autumn comes
When steeped in mellow sunlight
The fragile, golden leaves
Against a clear blue sky
Linger in the magic of the afternoon
And then reluctantly break off
And filter down to pave
A street with gold.
Then bare, gray branches
Lift themselves against the
Cold December sky
Sometimes weaving a web
Across the rose and dusk of late sunset
Sometimes against a frail new moon
And one bright star riding
A sky of that dark, living blue
Which comes before the heaviness
Of night descends, or the stars
Have powdered the heavens.
Winds beat against these trees;
The cold, but gentle rain of spring
Touches them lightly
The summer torrents strive
To lash them into a fury
And seek to break them—
But they stand.
My life is fevered
And a restlessness at times
An agony—again a vague
And baffling discontent
Possesses me.
I am thankful for my bit of sky
And trees, and for the shifting
Pageant of the seasons.
Such beauty lays upon the heart
A quiet.
Such eternal change and permanence
Take meaning from all turmoil

And leave serenity
Which knows no pain.

Brass Spittoons / LANGSTON HUGHES

Clean the spittoons, boy.
    Detroit,
    Chicago,
    Atlantic City,
    Palm Beach.
Clean the spittoons.
The steam in hotel kitchens,
And the smoke in hotel lobbies,
And the slime in hotel spittoons:
Part of my life.
    Hey, boy!
    A nickel,
    A dime,
    A dollar,
Two dollars a day.
    Hey, boy!
    A nickel,
    A dime,
    A dollar,
    Two dollars
Buy shoes for the baby.
House rent to pay.
Gin on Saturday,
Church on Sunday.
    My God!
Babies and gin and church
And women and Sunday

All mixed with dimes and
Dollars and clean spittoons
And house rent to pay.
  Hey, boy!
A bright bowl of brass is beautiful to the Lord.
Bright polished brass like the cymbals
Of King David's dancers,
Like the wine cups of Solomon.
  Hey, boy!
A clean spittoon on the altar of the Lord.
A clean bright spittoon all newly polished—
At least I can offer that.
  Com'mere, boy!

Cross / LANGSTON HUGHES

My old man's a white old man
And my old mother's black.
If ever I cursed my white old man
I take my curses back.

If ever I cursed my black old mother
And wished she were in hell,
I'm sorry for that evil wish
And now I wish her well.

My old man died in a fine big house.
My ma died in a shack.
I wonder where I'm gonna die,
Being neither white nor black?

Jazzonia / LANGSTON HUGHES

Oh, silver tree!
Oh, shining rivers of the soul.

In a Harlem cabaret
Six long-headed jazzers play.
A dancing girl whose eyes are bold
Lifts high a dress of silken gold.

Oh, singing tree!
Oh, shining rivers of the soul!

Were Eve's eyes
In the first garden
Just a bit too bold?
Was Cleopatra gorgeous
In a gown of gold?

Oh, shining tree!
Oh, silver rivers of the soul!

In a whirling cabaret
Six long-headed jazzers play.

The Negro Speaks of Rivers / LANGSTON HUGHES

I've known rivers:
I've known rivers ancient as the world and older than the
    flow of human blood in human veins.

My soul has grown deep like the rivers.

I bathed in the Euphrates when dawns were young.
I built my hut near the Congo and it lulled me to sleep.

I looked upon the Nile and raised the pyramids above it.
I heard the singing of the Mississippi when Abe Lincoln
   went down to New Orleans, and I've seen its muddy
   bosom turn all golden in the sunset.

I've known rivers:
Ancient, dusky rivers.

My soul has grown deep like the rivers.

I, Too / LANGSTON HUGHES

I, too, sing America.

I am the darker brother.
They send me to eat in the kitchen
When company comes,
But I laugh,
And eat well,
And grow strong.

Tomorrow,
I'll be at the table
When company comes.
Nobody'll dare
Say to me,
"Eat in the kitchen,"
Then.

Besides,
They'll see how beautiful I am
And be ashamed—

I, too, am America.

Bound No'th Blues / LANGSTON HUGHES

Goin' down the road, Lawd,
Goin' down the road.
Down the road, Lawd,
Way, way down the road.
Got to find somebody
To help me carry this load.

Road's in front o' me,
Nothin' to do but walk.
Road's in front o' me,
Walk . . . an' walk . . . an' walk.
I'd like to meet a good friend
To come along an' talk.

Hates to be lonely,
Lawd, I hates to be sad.
Says I hates to be lonely,
Hates to be lonely an' sad,
But ever' friend you finds seems
Like they try to do you bad.

Road, road, road, O!
Road, road . . . road . . . road, road!
Road, road, road, O!
On the no'thern road.
These Mississippi towns ain't
Fit fer a hoppin' toad.

Personal / LANGSTON HUGHES

In an envelope marked:
    PERSONAL
God addressed me a letter.
In an envelope marked:
    PERSONAL
I have given my answer.

Dream Variation / LANGSTON HUGHES

To fling my arms wide
In some place of the sun,
To whirl and to dance
Till the white day is done.
Then rest at cool evening
Beneath a tall tree
While night comes on gently,
    Dark like me—
That is my dream!

To fling my arms wide
In the face of the sun,
Dance! Whirl! Whirl!
Till the quick day is done.
Rest at pale evening . . .
A tall, slim tree . . .
Night coming tenderly
    Black like me.

Mother to Son / LANGSTON HUGHES

Well, son, I'll tell you:
Life for me ain't been no crystal stair.
It's had tacks in it,
And splinters,
And boards torn up,
And places with no carpet on the floor—
Bare.
But all the time
I'se been a-climbin' on,
And reachin' landin's,
And turnin' corners,
And sometimes goin' in the dark
Where there ain't been no light.
So boy, don't you turn back.
Don't you set down on the steps
'Cause you finds it's kinder hard.
Don't you fall now—
For I'se still goin', honey,
I'se still climbin',
And life for me ain't been no crystal stair.

Lenox Avenue Mural / LANGSTON HUGHES

HARLEM

What happens to a dream deferred?
    Does it dry up
    like a raisin in the sun?
    Or fester like a sore—
    And then run?

Does it stink like rotten meat?
Or crust and sugar over—
like a syrupy sweet?

Maybe it just sags
like a heavy load.

Or does it explode?

GOOD MORNING

Good morning, daddy!
I was born here, he said,
watched Harlem grow
until colored folks spread
from river to river
across the middle of Manhattan
out of Penn Station
dark tenth of a nation,
planes from Puerto Rico,
and holds of boats, chico,
up from Cuba Haiti Jamaica,
in busses marked New York
from Georgia Florida Louisiana
to Harlem Brooklyn the Bronx
but most of all to Harlem
dusky sash across Manhattan
I've seen them come dark
    wondering
    wide-eyed
    dreaming
out of Penn Station—
but the trains are late.
The gates open—
but there're bars
at each gate.
    What happens
    to a dream deferred?
Daddy, ain't you heard?

I said to my baby,
Baby, take it slow.
I can't, she said, I can't!
I got to go!
     There's a certain
     amount of traveling
     in a dream deferred.
Lulu said to Leonard,
I want a diamond ring.
Leonard said to Lulu,
You won't get a goddamn thing!
     A certain
     amount of nothing
     in a dream deferred.
Daddy, daddy, daddy,
All I want is you.
You can have me, baby—
but my lovin' days is through.
     A certain
     amount of impotence
     in a dream deferred.
Three parties
On my party line—
But that third party,
Lord, ain't mine!
     There's liable
     to be confusion
     in a dream deferred.
From river to river
Uptown and down,
There's liable to be confusion
when a dream gets kicked around.
     You talk like
     they don't kick
     dreams around
     Downtown.

I expect they do—
But I'm talking about
Harlem to you!

LETTER

Dear Mama,
        Time I pay rent and get my food
and laundry I don't have much left
but here is five dollars for you
to show you I still appreciates you.
My girl-friend send her love and say
she hopes to lay eyes on you sometime in life.
Mama, it has been raining cats and dogs up
here. Well, that is all so I will close.
        Your son baby
                Respectable as ever,
                        Joe

ISLAND

Between two rivers,
North of the park,
Like darker rivers
The streets are dark.

Black and white,
Gold and brown—
Chocolate-custard
Pie of a town.

Dream within a dream
Our dream deferred.

Good morning, daddy!

Ain't you heard?

Pennsylvania Station / LANGSTON HUGHES

The Pennsylvania Station in New York
Is like some vast basilica of old
That towers above the terrors of the dark
As bulwark and protection to the soul.
Now people who are hurrying alone
And those who come in crowds from far away
Pass through this great concourse of steel and stone
To trains, or else from trains out into day.
And as in great basilicas of old
The search was ever for a dream of God,
So here the search is still within each soul
Some seed to find that sprouts a holy tree
To glorify the earth—and you—and me.

I Dream a World / LANGSTON HUGHES

I dream a world where man
No other will scorn,
Where love will bless the earth
And peace its paths adorn.
I dream a world where all
Will know sweet freedom's way,
Where greed no longer saps the soul
Nor avarice blights our day.
A world I dream where black or white,
Whatever race you be,
Will share the bounties of the earth
And every man is free,
Where wretchedness will hang its head,

And joy, like a pearl,
Attend the needs of all mankind.
Of such I dream—
Our world!

Without Benefit of Declaration / LANGSTON HUGHES

Listen here, Joe
Don't you know
That tomorrow
You got to go
Out yonder where
The steel winds blow?

Listen here, kid,
It's been said
Tomorrow you'll be dead
Out there where
The snow is lead.

Don't ask me why.
Just go ahead and die.
Hidden from the sky
Out yonder you'll lie:
A medal to your family—
In exchange for
A guy.

Mama, don't cry.

Hatred / GWENDOLYN B. BENNETT

I shall hate you
Like a dart of singing steel
Shot through still air
At eventide.
Or solemnly
As pines are sober
When they stand etched
Against the sky.
Hating you shall be a game
Played with cool hands
And slim fingers.
Your heart will yearn
For the lonely splendor
Of the pine tree;
While rekindled fires
In my eyes
Shall wound you like swift arrows.
Memory will lay its hands
Upon your breast
And you will understand
My hatred.

Heritage / GWENDOLYN B. BENNETT

I want to see the slim palm trees,
Pulling at the clouds
With little pointed fingers. . . .

I want to see lithe Negro girls,
Etched dark against the sky
While sunset lingers.

I want to hear the silent sands,
Singing to the moon
Before the Sphinx-still face. . . .

I want to hear the chanting
Around a heathen fire
Of a strange black race.

I want to breathe the Lotus flow'r,
Sighing to the stars
With tendrils drinking at the Nile. . . .

I want to feel the surging
Of my sad people's soul
Hidden by a minstrel-smile.

Sonnet I / Gwendolyn B. Bennett

He came in silvern armor, trimmed with black—
A lover come from legends long ago—
With silver spurs and silken plumes a-blow,
And flashing sword aught fast and buckled back
In a carven sheat of Tamarack.
He came with footsteps beautifully slow,
And spoke in voice meticulously low.
He came and Romance followed in his track. . . .

I did not ask his name—I thought him Love;
I did not care to see his hidden face.
All life seemed born in my intaken breath;

All thought seemed flown like some forgotten dove.
He bent to kiss and raised his visor's lace . . .
All eager-lipped I kissed the mouth of Death.

Sonnet II / GWENDOLYN B. BENNETT

Some things are very dear to me—
Such things as flowers bathed by rain
Or patterns traced upon the sea
Or crocuses where snow has lain . . .
The iridescence of a gem,
The moon's cool opalescent light,
Azaleas and the scent of them,
And honeysuckles in the night.
And many sounds are also dear—
Like winds that sing among the trees
Or crickets calling from the weir
Or Negroes humming melodies.
But dearer far than all surmise
Are sudden tear-drops in your eyes.

A Black Man Talks of Reaping / ARNA BONTEMPS

I have sown beside all waters in my day.
I planted deep, within my heart the fear

75

That wind or fowl would take the grain away.
I planted safe against this stark, lean year.

I scattered seed enough to plant the land
In rows from Canada to Mexico,
But for my reaping only what the hand
Can hold at once is all that I can show.

Yet what I sowed and what the orchard yields
My brother's sons are gathering stalk and root,
Small wonder then my children glean in fields
They have not sown, and feed on bitter fruit.

Close Your Eyes! / ARNA BONTEMPS

Go through the gates with closed eyes.
Stand erect and let your black face front the west.
Drop the axe and leave the timber where it lies;
A woodman on the hill must have his rest.

Go where leaves are lying brown and wet.
Forget her warm arms and her breast who mothered you,
And every face you ever loved forget.
Close your eyes; walk bravely through.

The Day-Breakers / ARNA BONTEMPS

We are not come to wage a strife
    With swords upon this hill.

It is not wise to waste the life
   Against a stubborn will.
Yet would we die as some have done,
Beating a way for the rising sun.

Golgotha Is a Mountain / Arna Bontemps

Golgotha is a mountain, a purple mound
Almost out of sight.
One night they hanged two thieves there,
And another man.
Some women wept heavily that night;
Their tears are flowing still. They have made a river;
Once it covered me.
Then the people went away and left Golgotha
Deserted.
Oh, I've seen many mountains:
Pale purple mountains melting in the evening mists and
     blurring on the borders of the sky.
I climbed old Shasta and chilled my hands in its summer
     snows.
I rested in the shadow of Popocatepetl and it whispered to me
     of daring prowess.
I looked upon the Pyrenees and felt the zest of warm exotic
     nights.
I slept at the foot of Fujiyama and dreamed of legend and
     of death.
And I've seen other mountains rising from the wistful moors
     like the breasts of a slender maiden.
Who knows the mystery of mountains!
Some of them are awful, others are just lonely.

*   *   *

Italy has its Rome and California has San Francisco,
All covered with mountains.
Some think these mountains grew
Like ant hills
Or sand dunes.
That might be so—
I wonder what started them all!
Babylon is a mountain
And so is Ninevah,
With grass growing on them;
Palaces and hanging gardens started them.
I wonder what is under the hills
In Mexico
And Japan!
There are mountains in Africa, too.
Treasure is buried there:
Gold and precious stones
And moulded glory.
Lush grass is growing there
Sinking before the wind.
Black men are bowing
Naked in that grass
Digging with their fingers.
I am one of them:
Those mountains should be ours.
It would be great
To touch the pieces of glory with our hands.

These mute unhappy hills,
Bowed down with broken backs,
Speak often one to another:
"A day is as a year," they cry,
"And a thousand years as one day."
We watched the caravan
That bore our queen to the courts of Solomon;
And when the first slave traders came
We bowed our heads.
"Oh, Brothers, it is not long!

Dust shall yet devour the stones
But we shall be here when they are gone."
Mountains are rising all around me.
Some are so small they are not seen;
Others are large.
All of them get big in time and people forget
What started them at first.
Oh the world is covered with mountains!
Beneath each one there is something buried:
Some pile of wreckage that started it there.
Mountains are lonely and some are awful.

*   *   *

One day I will crumble.
They'll cover my heap with dirt and that will make a
        mountain.
I think it will be Golgotha.

Idolatry / ARNA BONTEMPS

You have been good to me, I give you this:
The arms of lovers empty as our own,
Marble lips sustaining one long kiss
And the hard sound of hammers breaking stone.

For I will build a chapel in the place
Where our love died and I will journey there
To make a sign and kneel before your face
And set an old bell tolling on the air.

Reconnaissance / ARNA BONTEMPS

After the cloud embankments,
The lamentation of wind,
And the starry descent into time,
We came to the flashing waters and shaded our eyes
From the glare.

Alone with the shore and the harbor,
The stems of the cocoanut trees,
The fronds of silence and hushed music,
We cried for the new revelation
And waited for miracles to rise.

Where elements touch and merge,
Where shadows swoon like outcasts on the sand
And the tired moment waits, its courage gone—
There were we

In latitudes where storms are born.

Southern Mansion / ARNA BONTEMPS

Poplars are standing there still as death
And ghosts of dead men
Meet their ladies walking
Two by two beneath the shade
And standing on the marble steps.

There is a sound of music echoing
Through the open door
And in the field there is

Another sound tinkling in the cotton:
Chains of bondmen dragging on the ground.

The years go back with an iron clank,
A hand is on the gate,
A dry leaf trembles on the wall.
Ghosts are walking.
They have broken roses down
And poplars stand there still as death.

Nocturne at Bethesda / ARNA BONTEMPS

I thought I saw an angel flying low,
I thought I saw the flicker of a wing
Above the mulberry trees; but not again.
Bethesda sleeps. This ancient pool that healed
A host of bearded Jews does not awake.

This pool that once the angels troubled does not move.
No angel stirs it now, no Saviour comes
With healing in His hands to rise the sick
And bid the lame man leap upon the ground.

The golden days are gone. Why do we wait
So long upon the marble steps, blood
Falling from our open wounds? and why
Do our black faces search the empty sky?
Is there something we have forgotten? some precious thing
We have lost, wandering in strange lands?

There was a day, I remember now,
I beat my breast and cried, "Wash me, God,
Wash me with a wave of wind upon
The barley; O quiet One, draw near, draw near!

Walk upon the hills with lovely feet
And in the waterfall stand and speak.

"Dip white hands in the lily pool and mourn
Upon the harps still hanging in the trees
Near Babylon along the river's edge,
But oh, remember me, I pray, before
The summer goes and rose leaves lose their red."

The old terror takes my heart, the fear
Of quiet waters and of faint twilights.
There will be better days when I am gone
And healing pools where I cannot be healed.
Fragrant stars will gleam forever and ever
Above the place where I lie desolate.

Yet I hope, still I long to live.
And if there can be returning after death
I shall come back. But it will not be here;
If you want me you must search for me
Beneath the palms of Africa. Or if
I am not there then you may call to me
Across the shining dunes, perhaps I shall
Be following a desert caravan.

I may pass through centuries of death
With quiet eyes, but I'll remember still
A jungle tree with burning scarlet birds.
There is something I have forgotten, some precious thing.
I shall be seeking ornaments of ivory,
I shall be dying for a jungle fruit.

                    You do not hear, Bethesda.
O still green water in a stagnant pool!
Love abandoned you and me alike.
There was a day you held a rich full moon
Upon your heart and listened to the words
Of men now dead and saw the angels fly.
There is a simple story on your face;

Years have wrinkled you. I know, Bethesda!
You are sad. It is the same with me.

Heritage (For Harold Jackman) / COUNTEE CULLEN

What is Africa to me:
Copper sun or scarlet sea,
Jungle star or jungle track,
Strong bronzed men, or regal black
Women from whose loins I sprang
When the birds of Eden sang?
One three centuries removed
From the scenes his fathers loved,
Spicy grove, cinnamon tree,
What is Africa to me?

So I lie, who all day long
Want no sound except the song
Sung by wild barbaric birds
Goading massive jungle herds,
Juggernauts of flesh that pass
Trampling tall defiant grass
Where young forest lovers lie,
Plighting troth beneath the sky.
So I lie, who always hear,
Though I cram against my ear
Both my thumbs, and keep them there,
Great drums throbbing through the air.
So I lie, whose fount of pride,
Dear distress, and joy allied,
Is my somber flesh and skin,
With the dark blood dammed within

Like great pulsing tides of wine
That, I fear, must burst the fine
Channels of the chafing net
Where they surge and foam and fret.

Africa? A book one thumbs
Listlessly, till slumber comes.
Unremembered are her bats
Circling through the night, her cats
Crouching in the river reeds,
Stalking gentle flesh that feeds
By the river brink; no more
Does the bugle-throated roar
Cry that monarch claws have leapt
From the scabbards where they slept.
Silver snakes that once a year
Doff the lovely coats you wear,
Seek no covert in your fear
Lest a mortal eye should see;
What's your nakedness to me?
Here no leprous flowers rear
Fierce corollas in the air;
Here no bodies sleek and wet,
Dripping mingled rain and sweat,
Tread the savage measures of
Jungle boys and girls in love.
What is last year's snow to me,
Last year's anything? The tree
Budding yearly must forget
How its past arose or set—
Bough and blossom, flower, fruit,
Even what shy bird with mute
Wonder at her travail there,
Meekly labored in its hair.
One three centuries removed
From the scenes his fathers loved,
Spicy grove, cinnamon tree,
What is Africa to me?

So I lie, who find no peace
Night or day, no slight release
From the unremittant beat
Made by cruel padded feet
Walking through my body's street.
Up and down they go, and back,
Treading out a jungle track.
So I lie, who never quite
Safely sleep from rain at night—
I can never rest at all
When the rain begins to fall;
Like a soul gone mad with pain
I must match its weird refrain;
Ever must I twist and squirm,
Writhing like a baited worm,
While its primal measures drip
Through my body, crying, "Strip!
Doff this new exuberance.
Come and dance the Lover's Dance!"
In an old remembered way
Rain works on me night and day.

Quaint, outlandish heathen gods
Black men fashion out of rods,
Clay, and brittle bits of stone,
In a likeness like their own,
My conversion came high-priced;
I belong to Jesus Christ,
Preacher of humility,
Heathen gods are naught to me.

Father, Son, and Holy Ghost,
So I make an idle boast;
Jesus of the twice-turned cheek,
Lamb of God, although I speak
With my mouth thus, in my heart
Do I play a double part.
Ever at Thy glowing altar
Must my heart grow sick and falter,

Wishing He I served were black,
Thinking then it would not lack
Precedent of pain to guide it,
Let who would or might deride it;
Surely then this flesh would know
Yours had borne a kindred woe.
Lord, I fashion dark gods, too,
Daring even to give You
Dark despairing features where,
Crowned with dark rebellious hair,
Patience wavers just so much as
Mortal grief compels, while touches
Quick and hot, of anger, rise
To smitten cheek and weary eyes.
Lord, forgive me if my need
Sometimes shapes a human creed.
All day long and all night through,
One thing only must I do:
Quench my pride and cool my blood,
Lest I perish in the flood,
Lest a hidden ember set
Timber that I thought was wet
Burning like the dryest flax,
Melting like the merest wax,
Lest the grave restore its dead.
Not yet has my heart or head
In the least way realized
They and I are civilized.

That Bright Chimeric Beast / COUNTEE CULLEN

That bright chimeric beast
Conceived yet never born,

86

Save in the poet's breast,
The white-flanked unicorn,
Never may be shaken
From his solitude;
Never may be taken
In any earthly wood.

That bird forever feathered,
Of its new self the sire,
After aeons weathered,
Reincarnate by fire,
Falcon may not nor eagle
Swerve from his eyrie,
Nor any crumb inveigle
Down to an earthly tree.

That fish of the dread regime
Invented to become
The fable and the dream
Of the Lord aquarium,
Leviathan, the jointed
Harpoon was never wrought
By which the Lord's anointed
Will suffer to be caught.

Bird of the deathless breast,
Fish of the frantic fin,
That bright chimeric beast
Flashing the argent skin,—
If beasts like these you'd harry,
Plumb then the poet's dream;
Make it your aviary,
Make it your wood and stream.

There only shall the swish
Be heard of the regal fish;
There like a golden knife
Dart the feet of the unicorn,
And there, death brought to life,
The dead bird be reborn.

Yet Do I Marvel / Countee Cullen

I doubt not God is good, well-meaning, kind,
And did He stoop to quibble could tell why
The little buried mole continues blind,
Why flesh that mirrors Him must someday die,
Make plain the reason tortured Tantalus
Is baited by the fickle fruit, declare
If merely brute caprice dooms Sisyphus
To struggle up a never-ending stair.
Inscrutable His ways are, and immune
To catechism by a mind too strewn
With petty cares to slightly understand
What awful brain compels His awful hand
Yet do I marvel at this curious thing:
To make a poet black, and bid him sing!

Four Epitaphs / Countee Cullen

1 FOR MY GRANDMOTHER

This lovely flower fell to seed;
Work gently sun and rain;
She held it as her dying creed
That she would grow again.

2 FOR JOHN KEATS, APOSTLE OF BEAUTY

Not writ in water nor in mist,
Sweet lyric throat, thy name.
Thy singing lips that cold death kissed
Have seared his own with flame.

3 FOR PAUL LAURENCE DUNBAR

Born of the sorrowful of heart
Mirth was a crown upon his head;
Pride kept his twisted lips apart
In jest, to hide a heart that bled.

4 FOR A LADY I KNOW

She even thinks that up in heaven
   Her class lies late and snores,
While poor black cherubs rise at seven
   To do celestial chores.

Simon the Cyrenian Speaks / COUNTEE CULLEN

He never spoke a word to me,
And yet He called my name;
He never gave a sign to me,
And yet I knew and came.

At first I said, "I will not bear
His cross upon my back;
He only seeks to place it there
Because my skin is black."

But He was dying for a dream,
And He was very meek,
And in His eyes there shone a gleam
Men journey far to seek.

It was Himself my pity bought;
I did for Christ alone
What all of Rome could not have wrought
With bruise of lash or stone.

Appoggiatura / Donald Jeffrey Hayes

It was water I was trying to think of all the time
Seeing the way you moved about the house. . . .
It was water, still and grey—or dusty blue
Where late at night the wind and a half-grown moon
Could make a crazy quilt of silver ripples
And it little mattered what you were about;
Whether painting in your rainbow-soiled smock
Or sitting by the window with the sunlight in your hair
That boiled like a golden cloud about your head
Or whether you sat in the shadows
Absorbed in the serious business
Of making strange white patterns with your fingers---
Whether it was any of these things
The emotion was always the same with me
And all the time it was water I was trying to recall,
Water, silent, breathless, restless,
Slowly rising, slowly falling, imperceptibly. . . .
It was the memory of water and the scent of air
Blown from the sea
That bothered me!

When you laughed, and that was so rare a festival,
I wanted to think of gulls dipping—
Grey wings, white-faced, into a rising wind
Dipping. . . .
Do you remember the day
You held a pale white flower to the sun
That I might see how the yellow rays
Played through the petals?
As I remember now
The flower was beautiful—
And the sunrays playing through—
And your slim fingers
And your tilting chin
But then:

There was only the indistinguishable sound of water silence;
The inaudible swish of one wave breaking. . . .

And now that you have moved on into the past,
You and your slim fingers
And your boiling hair,
Now that you have moved on into the past,
And I have time to stroll back through the corridors of
        memory,
It is like meeting an old friend at dawn
To find carved here deep in my mellowing mind
These words:
        "Sea-Woman—slim-fingered-water-thing. . . ."

Benediction / DONALD JEFFREY HAYES

Not with my hands
But with my heart I bless you:
May peace forever dwell
Within your breast!

May Truth's white light
Move with you and possess you—
And may your thoughts and words
Wear her bright crest!

May Time move down
Its endless path of beauty
Conscious of you
And better for your being!

Spring after Spring
Array itself in splendor

Seeking the favor
Of your sentient seeing!

May hills lean toward you,
Hills and windswept mountains,
And trees be happy
That have seen you pass—

Your eyes dark kinsmen
To the stars above you—
Your feet remembered
By the blades of grass . . . !

Haven / DONALD JEFFREY HAYES

I'll build a house of arrogance
A most peculiar inn
With only room for vanquished folk
With proud and tilted chin . . . !

Poet / DONALD JEFFREY HAYES

No rock along the road but knows
The inquisition of his toes;
No journey's end but what can say:
He paused and rested here a day!
No joy is there that you may meet
But what will say: His kiss was sweet!
No sorrow but will sob to you:
He knew me intimately too . . . !

Threnody / DONALD JEFFREY HAYES

Let happy throats be mute;
Only the tortured reed
Is made a flute!

Only the broken heart can sing
And make of song
A breathless and a lovely thing!

Only the sad—only the tortured throat
Contrives of sound
A strangely thrilling note!

Only the tortured throat can fling
Beauty against the sky—
Only the broken heart can sing
Not asking why . . . !

Alien / DONALD JEFFREY HAYES

Do not stifle me with the strange scent
Of low growing mountain lilies—
Do not confuse me
With the salubrious odor of honeysuckle!

I cannot separate in my mind
Sweetness from sweetness—
Mimosa from wild white violets;
Magnolia from Cape jasmine!

I am from north tide country,
I can understand only the scent of seaweed;

Salt marsh and scrub pine
Riding on the breath of an amorous fog!

O do not confuse me
With sweetness upon sweetness;
Let me escape safely from this gentle madness—
Let me go back to the salt of sanity
In the scent of the sea . . . !

Pastourelle / DONALD JEFFREY HAYES

Walk this mile in silence—
Let no sound intrude
Upon the vibrant stillness
Of this solitude!

Let no thought be spoken
Nor syllable be heard
Lest the spell be broken
By the thunder of a word!

Here such matchless wonder is
As might tear apart—
Should the lip give tone
To the fullness of the heart . . . !

The Resurrection / JONATHAN BROOKS

His friends went off and left Him dead
In Joseph's subterranean bed,
Embalmed with myrrh and sweet aloes,
And wrapped in snow-white burial clothes.

Then shrewd men came and set a seal
Upon His grave, lest thieves should steal
His lifeless form away, and claim
For Him an undeserving fame.

"There is no use," the soldiers said,
"Of standing sentries by the dead."
Wherefore, they drew their cloaks around
Themselves, and fell upon the ground,
And slept like dead men, all night through,
In the pale moonlight and chilling dew.

A muffled whiff of sudden breath
Ruffled the passive air of death.

He woke, and raised Himself in bed;
    Recalled how He was crucified;
Touched both hands' fingers to His head,
    And lightly felt His fresh-healed side.

Then with a deep, triumphant sigh,
He coolly put His grave-clothes by—
Folded the sweet, white winding sheet,
    The toweling, the linen bands,
    The napkin, all with careful hands—
And left the borrowed chamber neat.

His steps were like the breaking day:
    So soft across the watch He stole,
    He did not wake a single soul,
Nor spill one dewdrop by the way.

Now Calvary was loveliness:
  Lilies that flowered thereupon
Pulled off the white moon's pallid dress,
  And put the morning's vesture on.

"Why seek the living among the dead?
He is not here," the angel said.

The early winds took up the words,
And bore them to the lilting birds,
The leafing trees, and everything
That breathed the living breath of spring.

Flowers of Darkness / FRANK MARSHALL DAVIS

Slowly the night blooms, unfurling
Flowers of darkness, covering
The trellised sky, becoming
A bouquet of blackness
Unending
Touched with sprigs
Of pale and budding stars

Soft the night smell
Among April trees
Soft and richly rare
Yet commonplace
Perfume on a cosmic scale

I turn to you Mandy Lou
I see the flowering night
Cameo condensed
Into the lone black rose
Of your face

The young woman-smell
Of your poppy body
Rises to my brain as opium
Yet silently motionless
I sit with twitching fingers
Yea, even reverently
Sit I
With you and the blossoming night
For what flower, plucked,
Lingers long?

Four Glimpses of Night / FRANK MARSHALL DAVIS

I

Eagerly
Like a woman hurrying to her lover
Night comes to the room of the world
And lies, yielding and content
Against the cool round face
Of the moon.

II

Night is a curious child, wandering
Between earth and sky, creeping
In windows and doors, daubing
The entire neighborhood
With purple paint.
Day
Is an apologetic mother
Cloth in hand
Following after.

III

Peddling
From door to door
Night sells
Black bags of peppermint stars
Heaping cones of vanilla moon
Until
His wares are gone
Then shuffles homeward
Jingling the gray coins
Of daybreak.

IV

Night's brittle song, sliver-thin,
Shatters into a billion fragments
Of quiet shadows
At the blaring jazz
Of a morning sun.

No Images / WARING CUNEY

She does not know
Her beauty,
She thinks her brown body
Has no glory.

If she could dance
Naked,
Under palm trees
And see her image in the river
She would know.

But there are no palm trees
On the street,
And dishwater gives back no images.

Threnody / Waring Cuney

Only quiet death
Brings relief
From the wearisome
Interchange
Of hope and grief.
O body
(Credulous heart
And dream-torn head),
What will wisdom be
Or folly—
When you lie dead?
Life-beaten body
Bruised and sore—
Neither hunger nor satiety
Are known beyond death's door.

Finis / Waring Cuney

Now that our love has drifted
To a quiet close,
Leaving the empty ache
That always follows when beauty goes;
Now that you and I,
Who stood tiptoe on earth
To touch our fingers to the sky,
Have turned away
To allow our little love to die—
Go, dear, seek again the magic touch.
But if you are wise,
As I shall be wise,
You will not again
Love overmuch.

Poem / Helene Johnson

Little brown boy,
Slim, dark, big-eyed,
Crooning love songs to your banjo
Down at the Lafayette—
Gee, boy, I love the way you hold your head,
High sort of and a bit to one side,
Like a prince, a jazz prince. And I love
Your eyes flashing, and your hands,
And your patent-leathered feet,
And your shoulders jerking the jig-wa.
And I love your teeth flashing,

And the way your hair shines in the spotlight
Like it was the real stuff.
Gee, brown boy, I loves you all over.
I'm glad I'm a jig. I'm glad I can
Understand your dancin' and your
Singin', and feel all the happiness
And joy and don't-care in you.
Gee, boy, when you sing, I can close my ears
And hear tom-toms just as plain.
Listen to me, will you, what do I know
About tom-toms? But I like the word, sort of,
Don't you? It belongs to us.
Gee, boy, I love the way you hold your head,
And the way you sing and dance,
And everything.
Say, I think you're wonderful. You're
All right with me,
You are.

The Road / HELENE JOHNSON

Ah, little road, all whirry in the breeze,
A leaping clay hill lost among the trees,
The bleeding note of rapture-streaming thrush
Caught in a drowsy bush
And stretched out in a single singing line of dusky song.
Ah, little road, brown as my race is brown,
Your trodden beauty like our trodden pride,
Dust of the dust, they must not bruise you down.
Rise to one brimming golden, spilling cry!

Sonnet to a Negro in Harlem / HELENE JOHNSON

You are disdainful and magnificent—
Your perfect body and your pompous gait,
Your dark eyes flashing solemnly with hate,
Small wonder that you are incompetent
To imitate those whom you so despise—
Your shoulders towering high above the throng,
Your head thrown back in rich, barbaric song,
Palm trees and mangoes stretched before your eyes.
Let others toil and sweat for labor's sake
And wring from grasping hands their meed of gold.
Why urge ahead your supercilious feet?
Scorn will efface each footprint that you make.
I love your laughter arrogant and bold.
You are too splendid for this city street.

Invocation / HELENE JOHNSON

Let me be buried in the rain
In a deep, dripping wood,
Under the warm wet breast of Earth
Where once a gnarled tree stood.
And paint a picture on my tomb
With dirt and a piece of bough
Of a girl and a boy beneath a round, ripe moon
Eating of love with an eager spoon
And vowing an eager vow.
And do not keep my plot mowed smooth
And clean as a spinster's bed,
But let the weed, the flower, the tree,
Riotous, rampant, wild, and free,
Grow high above my head.

Between the World and Me / RICHARD WRIGHT

And one morning while in the woods I stumbled suddenly
    upon the thing,
Stumbled upon it in a grassy clearing guarded by scaly oaks
    and elms.
And the sooty details of the scene rose, thrusting themselves
    between the world and me. . . .

There was a design of white bones slumbering forgottenly
    upon a cushion of ashes.
There was a charred stump of a sapling pointing a blunt
    finger accusingly at the sky.
There were torn tree limbs, tiny veins of burnt leaves, and a
    scorched coil of greasy hemp;
A vacant shoe, an empty tie, a ripped shirt, a lonely hat, and
    a pair of trousers stiff with black blood.
And upon the trampled grass were buttons, dead matches,
    butt-ends of cigars and cigarettes, peanut shells, a
    drained gin-flask, and a whore's lipstick;
Scattered traces of tar, restless arrays of feathers, and the
    lingering smell of gasoline.
And through the morning air the sun poured yellow surprise
    into the eye sockets of a stony skull. . . .
And while I stood my mind was frozen with a cold pity for
    the life that was gone.
The ground gripped my feet and my heart was circled by
    icy walls of fear—
The sun died in the sky; a night wind muttered in the grass
    and fumbled the leaves in the trees; the woods poured
    forth the hungry yelping of hounds; the darkness
    screamed with thirsty voices; and the witnesses rose
    and lived:
The dry bones stirred, rattled, lifted, melting themselves into
    my bones.
The grey ashes formed flesh firm and black, entering into my
    flesh.

The gin-flask passed from mouth to mouth; cigars and ciga-
rettes glowed, the whore smeared the lipstick red
upon her lips,
And a thousand faces swirled around me, clamoring that
my life be burned. . . .

And then they had me, stripped me, battering my teeth into
my throat till I swallowed my own blood.
My voice was drowned in the roar of their voices, and my
black wet body slipped and rolled in their hands as
they bound me to the sapling.
And my skin clung to the bubbling hot tar, falling from me in
limp patches.
And the down and quills of the white feathers sank into my
raw flesh, and I moaned in my agony.
Then my blood was cooled mercifully, cooled by a baptism
of gasoline.
And in a blaze of red I leaped to the sky as pain rose like
water, boiling my limbs.
Panting, begging I clutched childlike, clutched to the hot
sides of death.
Now I am dry bones and my face a stony skull staring in
yellow surprise at the sun. . . .

Hokku Poems / RICHARD WRIGHT

I am nobody
A red sinking autumn sun
Took my name away

Make up your mind snail!
You are half inside your house
And halfway out!

In the falling snow
A laughing boy holds out his palms
Until they are white

Keep straight down this block
Then turn right where you will find
A peach tree blooming

With a twitching nose
A dog reads a telegram
On a wet tree trunk

The spring lingers on
In the scent of a damp log
Rotting in the sun

Whose town did you leave
O wild and drowning spring rain
And where do you go?

The crow flew so fast
That he left his lonely caw
Behind in the fields

Adjuration / CHARLES ENOCH WHEELER

Let the knowing speak,
Let the oppressed tell of their sorrows,
Of their salt and boundless grief.
Since even the wise and the brave
Must wonder, and the creeping mists
Of doubt, creep along the trough
Of pursuing woe . . .
To curl among the crevices

Of the most cannily armored brain.
Let those who can endure their doubts
Speak for the comfort of the weary
Who weep to know.

Without Name / Pauli Murray

Call it neither love nor spring madness,
Nor chance encounter nor quest ended.
Observe it casually as pussy willows
Or pushcart pansies on a city street.
Let this seed growing in us
Granite-strong with persistent root
Be without name, or call it the first
Warm wind that caressed your cheek
And traded unshared kisses between us.
Call it the elemental earth
Bursting the clasp of too-long winter
And trembling for the plough-blade.

Let our blood chant it
And our flesh sing anthems to its arrival,
But our lips shall be silent, uncommitted.

Dark Testament / Pauli Murray

Hope is a crushed stalk
Between clenched fingers.
Hope is a bird's wing
Broken by a stone.
Hope is a word in a tuneless ditty—
A word whispered with the wind,
A dream of forty acres and a mule,
A cabin of one's own and rest days often
A name and place for one's children
And children's children at last . . .
Hope is a song in a weary throat.

> *O give me a song of hope*
> *And a world where I can sing it.*
> *Give me a song of faith*
> *And a people to believe in it.*
> *Give me a song of kindliness*
> *And a country where I can live it.*
> *O give me a song of hope and love*
> *And a brown girl's heart to hear it.*

*   *   *

Tear it out of the history books!
Bury it in conspiracies of silence!
Fight many wars to suppress it!
But it is written in our faces
Twenty million times over!
It sings in our blood,
It cries from the housetops,
It mourns with the wind in the forests,
When dogs howl and will not be comforted,
When newborn lambs bleat in the snowdrifts,
And dead leaves rattle in the graveyards.

And we'll shout it from the mountains,
We'll tell it in the valleys,
We'll talk it in miner's shack,
We'll sing it at the work bench,
We'll whisper it over back fences.
We'll speak it in the kitchen,
We'll state it at the White House,
We'll tell it everywhere to all who will listen—

We will lay siege, let thunder serve our claim,
For it must be told, endlessly told, and you must hear it.
Listen, white brothers, hear the dirge of history,
And hold out your hand—Hold out your hand.

*   *   *

Of us who darkly stand
Bared to the spittle of every curse,
Nor left the dignity of beasts,
Let none say,
"Those were not men but cowards all,
With eyes dull-lidded as a frog's.
They labored long but not from love,
Striving from blind perpetual fear."

Better our seed rot on the ground
And our hearts burn to ash
Than the years be empty of our imprint,
We have no other dream, no land but this.
With slow deliberate hands these years
Have set her image on our brows.
We are her seed, have borne a fruit
Native and pure as unblemished cotton.

Then let the dream linger on.
Let it be the test of nations,
Let it be the quest of all our days,
The fevered pounding of our blood,
The measure of our souls,—
That none shall rest in any land

And none return to dreamless sleep,
No heart be quieted, no tongue be stilled
Until the final man may stand in any place
And thrust his shoulders to the sky,
Friend and brother to every other man.

A Ballad of Remembrance / ROBERT HAYDEN

Quadroon mermaids, Afro angels, black saints
balanced upon the switchblades of that air
and sang. Tight streets unfolding to the eye
like fans of corrosion and elegiac lace
crackled with their singing: Shadow of time. Shadow of
    blood.

Shadow, echoed the Zulu king, dangling
from a cluster of balloons. Blood,
whined the gun-metal priestess, floating
over the courtyard where dead men diced.

What will you have? she inquired, the sallow vendeuse
of prepared tarnishes and jokes of nacre and ormolu,
what but those gleamings, oldrose graces,
manners like scented gloves? Contrived ghosts
rapped to metronome clack of lavalieres.

Contrived illuminations riding a threat
of river, masked Negroes wearing chameleon
satins gaudy now as a fortuneteller's
dream of disaster, lighted the crazy flopping
dance of love and hate among joys, rejections.

Accommodate, muttered the Zulu king,
toad on a throne of glaucous poison jewels.

Love, chimed the saints and the angels and the mermaids.
Hate, shrieked the gun-metal priestess
from her spiked bellcollar curved like a fleur-de-lis:

As well have a talon as a finger, a muzzle as a mouth,
as well have a hollow as a heart. And she pinwheeled
away in coruscations of laughter, scattering
those others before her like foil stars.

But the dance continued—now among metaphorical
doors, coffee cups floating poised
hysterias, decors of illusion; now among
mazurka dolls offering death's-heads
of cocaine roses and real violets.

Then you arrived, meditative, ironic,
richly human; and your presence was shore where I rested
released from the hoodoo of that dance, where I spoke
with my true voice again.

And therefore this is not only a ballad of remembrance
for the down-South arcane city with death
in its jaws like gold teeth and archaic cusswords;
not only a token for the troubled generous friends
held in the fists of that schizoid city like flowers,
but also, Mark Van Doren,
a poem of remembrance, a gift, a souvenir for you

Witch Doctor / ROBERT HAYDEN

I

He dines alone surrounded by reflections
of himself. Then after sleep and benzedrine
descends the Cinquecento stair his magic

wrought from hypochondria of the well-
to-do and nagging deathwish of the poor;
swirls on smiling genuflections of
his liveried chauffeur into a crested
lilac limousine, the cynosure
of mousey neighbors tittering behind
Venetian blinds and half afraid of him
and half admiring his outrageous flair.

II

Meanwhile his mother, priestess in gold lamé,
precedes him to the quondam theater
now Israel Temple of the Highest Alpha,
where the bored, the sick, the alien, the tired
await euphoria. With deadly vigor
she prepares the way for mystery
and lucre. Shouts in blues-contralto, "He's
God's dictaphone of all-redeeming truth.
Oh he's the holyweight champeen who's come
to give the knockout lick to your bad luck;
say he's the holyweight champeen who's here
to deal a knockout punch to your hard luck."

III

Reposing on cushions of black leopard skin,
he telephones instructions for a long
slow drive across the park that burgeons now
with spring and sailors. Peers questingly
into the green, fountainous twilight, sighs
and turns the gold-plate dial to Music For
Your Dining-Dancing Pleasure. Smoking Egyptian
cigarettes rehearses in his mind
a new device that he must use tonight.

IV

Approaching Israel Temple, mask in place,
he hears ragtime allegros of a "Song

111

of Zion" that becomes, when he appears,
a hallelujah wave for him to walk.
His mother and a rainbow-surpliced cordon
conduct him choiring to the altar-stage,
and there he kneels and seems to pray before
a lighted Jesus painted sealskin-brown.
Then with a glittering flourish he arises,
turns, gracefully extends his draperied arms:
"Israelites, true Jews, O found lost tribe
of Israel, receive my blessing now.
Selah, selah." He feels them yearn toward him
as toward a lover, exults before the image
of himself their trust gives back. Stands as though
in meditation, letting their eyes caress
his garments jewelled and chatoyant, cut
to fall, to flow from his tall figure
dramatically just so. Then all at once
he sways, quivers, gesticulates as if
to ward off blows or kisses, and when he speaks
again he utters wildering vocables,
hypnotic no-words planned (and never failing)
to enmesh his flock in theopathic tension.
Cries of eudaemonic pain attest
his artistry. Behind the mask he smiles.
And now in subtly altering light he chants
and sinuously trembles, chants and trembles
while convulsive energies of eager faith
surcharge the theater with power of
their own, a power he has counted on
and for a space allows to carry him.
Dishevelled antiphons proclaim the moment
his followers all day have hungered for,
but which is his alone.
He signals: tambourines begin, frenetic
drumbeat and glissando. He dances from the altar,
robes hissing, flaring, shimmering; down aisles
where mantled guardsmen intercept wild hands
that arduously strain to clutch his vestments,

he dances, dances, ensorcelled and aloof,
the fervid juba of God as lover, healer,
conjurer. And of himself as God.

Middle Passage / ROBERT HAYDEN

I

Jesús, Estrella, Esperanza, Mercy:

Sails flashing to the wind like weapons,
sharks following the moans the fever and the dying;
horror the corposant and compass rose.

Middle Passage:
          voyage through death
                    to life upon these shores.

"10 April 1800—
Blacks rebellious. Crew uneasy. Our linguist says
their moaning is a prayer for death,
ours and their own. Some try to starve themselves.
Lost three this morning leaped with crazy laughter
to the waiting sharks, sang as they went under."

Desire, Adventure, Tartar, Ann:

Standing to America, bringing home
black gold, black ivory, black seed.

  *Deep in the festering hold thy father lies,
  of his bones New England pews are made,
  those are altar lights that were his eyes.*

Jesus   Saviour   Pilot   Me
Over   Life's   Tempestuous   Sea

We pray that Thou wilt grant, O Lord,
safe passage to our vessels bringing
heathen souls unto Thy chastening.

Jesus   Saviour

> "8 bells. I cannot sleep, for I am sick
> with fear, but writing eases fear a little
> since still my eyes can see these words take shape
> upon the page & so I write, as one
> would turn to exorcism. 4 days scudding,
> but now the sea is calm again. Misfortune
> follows in our wake like sharks (our grinning
> tutelary gods). Which one of us
> has killed an albatross? A plague among
> our blacks—Ophthalmia: blindness—& we
> have jettisoned the blind to no avail.
> It spreads, the terrifying sickness spreads.
> Its claws have scratched sight from the Capt.'s eyes
> & there is blindness in the fo'c'sle
> & we must sail 3 weeks before we come
> to port."

> *What port awaits us, Davy Jones'*
> *or home? I've heard of slavers drifting, drifting,*
> *playthings of wind and storm and chance, their*
> > *crews*
> *gone blind, the jungle hatred*
> *crawling up on deck.*

Thou   Who   Walked   On   Galilee

> "Deponent further sayeth *The Bella J*
> left the Guinea Coast
> with cargo of five hundred blacks and odd
> for the barracoons of Florida:

114

"That there was hardly room 'tween-decks for half
the sweltering cattle stowed spoon-fashion there;
that some went mad of thirst and tore their flesh
and sucked the blood:

"That Crew and Captain lusted with the comeliest
of the savage girls kept naked in the cabins;
that there was one they called The Guinea Rose
and they cast lots and fought to lie with her:

"That when the Bo's'n piped all hands, the flames
spreading from starboard already were beyond
control, the Negroes howling and their chains
entangled with the flames:

"That the burning blacks could not be reached,
that the Crew abandoned ship,
leaving their shrieking Negresses behind,
that the Captain perished drunken with the wenches:

"Further Deponent sayeth not."

Pilot   Oh   Pilot   Me

II

Aye, lad, and I have seen those factories,
Gambia, Rio Pongo, Calabar;
have watched the artful mongos baiting traps
of war wherein the victor and the vanquished

Were caught as prizes for our barracoons.
Have seen the nigger kings whose vanity
and greed turned wild black hides of Fellatah,
Mandingo, Ibo, Kru to gold for us.

And there was one—King Anthracite we named him—
fetish face beneath French parasols
of brass and orange velvet, impudent mouth
whose cups were carven skulls of enemies:

He'd honor us with drum and feast and conjo
and palm-oil-glistening wenches deft in love,

and for tin crowns that shone with paste,
red calico and German-silver trinkets.

Would have the drums talk war and send
his warriors to burn the sleeping villages
and kill the sick and old and lead the young
in coffles to our factories.

Twenty years a trader, twenty years,
for there was wealth aplenty to be harvested
from those black fields, and I'd be trading still
but for the fevers melting down my bones.

III

Shuttles in the rocking loom of history,
the dark ships move, the dark ships move,
their bright ironical names
like jests of kindness on a murderer's mouth;
plough through thrashing glister toward
fata morgana's lucent melting shore,
weave toward New World littorals that are
mirage and myth and actual shore.

Voyage through death,
                                        voyage whose chartings are unlove

A charnel stench, effluvium of living death
spreads outward from the hold,
where the living and the dead, the horribly dying,
lie interlocked, lie foul with blood and excrement.

> *Deep in the festering hold thy father lies,*
> *the corpse of mercy rots with him,*
> *rats eat love's rotten gelid eyes.*

> *But, oh, the living look at you*
> *with human eyes whose suffering accuses you,*
> *whose hatred reaches through the swill of dark*
> *to strike you like a leper's claw.*

You cannot stare that hatred down
or chain the fear that stalks the watches
and breathes on you its fetid scorching breath;
cannot kill the deep immortal human wish,
the timeless will.

"But for the storm that flung up barriers
of wind and wave, *The Amistad*, señores,
would have reached the port of Príncipe in two,
three days at most; but for the storm we should
have been prepared for what befell.
Swift as the puma's leap it came. There was
that interval of moonless calm filled only
with the water's and the rigging's usual sounds,
then sudden movement, blows and snarling cries
and they had fallen on us with machete
and marlinspike. It was as though the very
air, the night itself were striking us.
Exhausted by the rigors of the storm,
we were no match for them. Our men went down
before the murderous Africans. Our loyal
Celestino ran from below with gun
and lantern and I saw, before the cane-
knife's wounding flash, Cinquez,
that surly brute who calls himself a prince,
directing, urging on the ghastly work.
He hacked the poor mulatto down, and then
he turned on me. The decks were slippery
when daylight finally came. It sickens me
to think of what I saw, of how these apes
threw overboard the butchered bodies of
our men, true Christians all, like so much jetsam.
Enough, enough. The rest is quickly told:
Cinquez was forced to spare the two of us
you see to steer the ship to Africa,
and we like phantoms doomed to rove the sea
voyaged east by day and west by night,
deceiving them, hoping for rescue,

prisoners on our own vessel, till
at length we drifted to the shores of this
your land, America, where we were freed
from our unspeakable misery. Now we
demand, good sirs, the extradition of
Cinquez and his accomplices to La
Havana. And it distresses us to know
there are so many here who seem inclined
to justify the mutiny of these blacks.
We find it paradoxical indeed
that you whose wealth, whose tree of liberty
are rooted in the labor of your slaves
should suffer the august John Quincy Adams
to speak with so much passion of the right
of chattel slaves to kill their lawful masters
and with his Roman rhetoric weave a hero's
garland for Cinquez. I tell you that
we are determined to return to Cuba
with our slaves and there see justice done.
   Cinquez—
or let us say 'the Prince'—Cinquez shall die."

The deep immortal human wish,
the timeless will:

  Cinquez its deathless primaveral image,
  life that transfigures many lives.

Voyage through death
       to life upon these shores.

Frederick Douglass / ROBERT HAYDEN

When it is finally ours, this freedom, this liberty, this
        beautiful
and terrible thing, needful to man as air,
usable as earth; when it belongs at last to our children,
when it is truly instinct, brain matter, diastole, systole,
reflex action; when it is finally won; when it is more
than the gaudy mumbo jumbo of politicians:
this man, this Douglass, this former slave, this Negro
beaten to his knees, exiled, visioning a world
where none is lonely, none hunted, alien,
this man, superb in love and logic, this man
shall be remembered. Oh, not with statues' rhetoric,
not with legends and poems and wreaths of bronze alone,
but with the lives grown out of his life, the lives
fleshing his dream of the beautiful, needful thing.

Veracruz / ROBERT HAYDEN

I

Sunday afternoon,
and couples walk the breakwater
heedless of the bickering spray.
Near the shoreward end,
Indian boys idle and fish.
A shawled brown woman
squinting against
the ricocheting brilliance
of sun and water

119

shades her eyes and gazes
toward the fort,
fossil of Spanish power,
looming in the harbor.

At the seaward end,
a pharos like a temple rises.
From here the shore
seen across marbling waves
is arabesque ornately green
that hides the inward-falling slum,
the stains and dirty tools of struggle;
appears a destination dreamed of,
never to be reached.

Here only the sea is real—
the barbarous multifoliate sea
with its rustlings of leaves,
fire, garments, wind;
its clashing of phantasmal jewels,
its lunar thunder,
animal and human sighing.

Leap now,
and cease from error.
Escape. Or shoreward turn,
accepting all—
the losses and farewells,
the long warfare with self,
with God.

The waves roar in and break
roar in and break
with granite spreeing hiss
on bronzegreen rocks below
and glistering upfling of spray

II

Thus reality
   bedizened in the warring colors
      of a dream
parades through these
   arcades ornate with music and
      the sea.

Thus reality
   become unbearably a dream
      beckons
out of reach in flyblown streets
   of lapsing rose and purple, dying
      blue.

Thus marimba'd night
   and multifoliate sea become
      phantasmal
space, and there,
   light-years away, one farewell image
      burns and fades and burns.

Perspectives / DUDLEY RANDALL

Futile to chide the stinging shower
Or prosecute the thorn
Or set a curse upon the hour
In which my love was born.

All's done, all's vanished, like a sail
That's dwindled down the bay.
Even the mountains vast and tall
The sea dissolves away.

I Loved You Once (From the Russian of Alexander Pushkin) / DUDLEY RANDALL

I loved you once; love even yet, it may be,
Within my soul has not quite died away;
But let that cause you no anxiety;
I would not give you pain in any way.
I loved you helplessly, and hopelessly,
With jealousy, timidity, brought low;
I loved you so intensely, tenderly,
I pray to God another love you so.

Sorrow Is the Only Faithful One / OWEN DODSON

Sorrow is the only faithful one:
The lone companion clinging like a season
To its original skin no matter what the variations.

If all the mountains paraded
Eating the valleys as they went
And the sun were a cliffure on the highest peak,

Sorrow would be there between
The sparkling and the giant laughter
Of the enemy when the clouds come down to swim.

But I am less, unmagic, black,
Sorrow clings to me more than to doomsday mountains
Or erosion scars on a palisade.

Sorrow has a song like a leech
Crying because the sand's blood is dry
And the stars reflected in the lake

122

Are water for all their twinkling
And bloodless for all their charm.
I have blood, and a song.
SORROW IS THE ONLY FAITHFUL ONE.

Drunken Lover / OWEN DODSON

This is the stagnant hour:
The dead communion between mouth and mouth,
The drunken kiss lingered,
The dreadful equator south.

This is the hour of impotence
When the unfulfilled is unfulfilled.
Only the stale breath is anxious
And warm. All else is stilled.

Why did I come to this reek,
This numb time, this level?
Only for you, my love, only for you
Could I endure this devil.

I dreamed when I was
A pimply and urgent adolescent
Of these hours when love would be fire
And you the steep descent.

My mouth's inside is like cotton,
Your arm is dead on my arm,
What I pictured so lovely and spring
Is August and fungus calm.

O lover, draw away, grow small, go magic,
O lover, disappear into the tick of this bed;
Open all the windows to the north
For the wind to cool my head.

Sickle Pears (For Glidden Parker) / OWEN DODSON

In college once I climbed the tree
With sickle pears our Greek professor loved.
High in that natural world I shook
An Autumn down;

A tumble of roughed fruit
Bounced onto the cider ground.
Fell to my waiting friend.

Together we went on to maple meadows
To celebrate the harvest of the year.
By chewing sickle pears we won a year:
Digesting all he planted thought by thought
From early Homer to the precious here.

Hymn Written After Jeremiah Preached to Me in a Dream / OWEN DODSON

Nowhere are we safe.
Surely not in love,
Morning ripe at three
Or in the Holy Trinity.

(My God, look after me.)

Where does Grace abide,
Whole, whole in surety?
Or does sin abide
Where virtue tries, in shame, to hide?

(My God, have I no pride?)

Shall I try the whole,
Crippled in my will,
Spatter where it falls
My carnal-fire waterfalls?

(My angel, in compassion, calls.)

Secret, knotted shame
Rips me like a curse.
Unction in my dust
Gives me final thrust.

(My God, consider dust!)

Yardbird's Skull (For Charlie Parker) / OWEN DODSON

The bird is lost,
Dead, with all the music:
Whole sunsets heard the brain's music
Faded to last horizon notes.
I do not know why I hold
This skull, smaller than a walnut's,
Against my ear,
Expecting to hear
The smashed fear
Of childhood from . . . bone;
Expecting to see
Wind nosing red and purple,
Strange gold and magic
On bubbled windowpanes
Of childhood. Shall I hear?
I should hear: this skull
Has been with violets

Not Yorick, or the gravedigger,
Yapping his yelling story,
This skull has been in air,
Sensed his brother, the swallow,
(Its talent for snow and crumbs).
Flown to lost Atlantis islands,
Places of dreaming, swimming lemmings.
O I shall hear skull skull,
Hear your lame music,
Believe music rejects undertaking,
Limps back.
Remember tiny lasting, we get lonely:
Come sing, come sing, come sing sing
And sing.

Sailors on Leave / Owen Dodson

No boy chooses war.
Dear let me show
The picket fence
Around my heart
Where loves are hung
In pairs of pain
And joy: the piercing revellers.

Here in this bar, the Cosycue,
I hear my darling singer moan,
Lower lights within my mind,
Admit a surer light
To see, to die by.

Here so specially set
For me, I am amazed,

Are target lovers all lines
For me to break,
To leave them, to die by.

No boy chooses war
But then we go
And in a cause find causes
To regret the summer and
The easy girl or boy
We drift to exist,
To battle for, to die.

Stevedore / LESLIE M. COLLINS

The enigmatic moon has at long last died.
Even as the ancient Cathedral Saint Louis
Peals her lazy call
To a sleepy solemn worship,
Night's mysterious shadows reveal their secrets
And rise into nothingness
As honest day unfurls her bright banners.

The stevedore,
Sleep spilled on his black face,
Braves the morning's rising fog,
The saturating chill.

As the sun burns itself out in summer brilliance,
Though his heart he sweated out
In water glistening from gargantuan shoulders,
He finds strength in his voice,
Singing of Moses down in Egyptland,
Of yesterday's untrue love.

127

By evening
The sun-scorched stevedore has packed strange cargoes
On alien ships
Whose destinations stir no romantic desires.

All day
A little of his soul is put to sea.
And now that the heaven's sun-burnt gold
Has quickened to deepest lapis-lazuli,
He turns an unkempt head

Homeward
To a dreamless slumber.

For My People / Margaret Walker

For my people everywhere singing their slave songs re-
       peatedly: their dirges and their ditties and their blues
       and jubilees, praying their prayers nightly to an un-
       known god, bending their knees humbly to an unseen
       power;
For my people lending their strength to the years: to the
       gone years and the now years and the maybe years,
       washing ironing cooking scrubbing sewing mending
       hoeing plowing digging planting pruning patching
       dragging along never gaining never reaping never
       knowing and never understanding;
For my playmates in the clay and dust and sand of Alabama
       backyards playing baptizing and preaching, and doc-
       tor and jail and soldier and school and mama and
       cooking and playhouse and concert and store and
       Miss Choomby and hair and company;

For the cramped bewildered years we went to school to
	learn to know the reasons why and the answers to and
	the people who and the places where and the days
	when, in memory of the bitter hours when we discov-
	ered we were black and poor and small and different
	and nobody wondered and nobody understood;
For the boys and girls who grew in spite of these things to
	be Man and Woman, to laugh and dance and sing and
	play and drink their wine and religion and success, to
	marry their playmates and bear children and then die
	of consumption and anemia and lynching;
For my people thronging 47th Street in Chicago and Lenox
	Avenue in New York and Rampart Street in New Or-
	leans, lost disinherited dispossessed and HAPPY peo-
	ple filling the cabarets and taverns and other people's
	pockets needing bread and shoes and milk and land
	and money and Something—Something all our own;
For my people walking blindly, spreading joy, losing time
	being lazy, sleeping when hungry, shouting when bur-
	dened, drinking when hopeless, tied and shackled and
	tangled among ourselves by the unseen creatures who
	tower over us omnisciently and laugh;
For my people blundering and groping and floundering in
	the dark of churches and schools and clubs and so-
	cieties, associations and councils and committees and
	conventions, distressed and disturbed and deceived
	and devoured by money-hungry glory-craving leeches,
	preyed on by facile force of state and fad and novelty
	by false prophet and holy believer;
For my people standing staring trying to fashion a better
	way from confusion from hypocrisy and misunder-
	standing, trying to fashion a world that will hold all
	the people all the faces all the adams and eves and
	their countless generations;
Let a new earth rise. Let another world be born. Let a bloody
	peace be written in the sky. Let a second generation
	full of courage issue forth, let a people loving freedom
	come to growth, let a beauty full of healing and a

strength of final clenching be the pulsing in our spirits and our blood. Let the martial songs be written, let the dirges disappear. Let a race of men now rise and take control!

Molly Means / MARGARET WALKER

Old Molly Means was a hag and a witch;
Chile of the devil, the dark, and sitch.
Her heavy hair hung thick in ropes
And her blazing eyes was black as pitch.
Imp at three and wench at 'leben
She counted her husbands to the number seben.
    O Molly, Molly, Molly Means
    There goes the ghost of Molly Means.

Some say she was born with a veil on her face
So she could look through unnatchal space
Through the future and through the past
And charm a body or an evil place
And every man could well despise
The evil look in her coal black eyes.
    Old Molly, Molly, Molly Means
    Dark is the ghost of Molly Means.

And when the tale begun to spread
Of evil and of holy dread:
Her black-hand arts and her evil powers
How she cast her spells and called the dead,
The younguns was afraid at night
And the farmers feared their crops would blight.
    Old Molly, Molly, Molly Means
    Cold is the ghost of Molly Means.

Then one dark day she put a spell
On a young gal-bride just come to dwell
In the lane just down from Molly's shack
And when her husband come riding back
His wife was barking like a dog
And on all fours like a common hog.
     O Molly, Molly, Molly Means
     Where is the ghost of Molly Means?

The neighbors come and they went away
And said she'd die before break of day
But her husband held her in his arms
And swore he'd break the wicked charms;
He'd search all up and down the land
And turn the spell on Molly's hand.
     O Molly, Molly, Molly Means
     Sharp is the ghost of Molly Means.

So he rode all day and he rode all night
And at the dawn he come in sight
Of a man who said he could move the spell
And cause the awful thing to dwell
On Molly Means, to bark and bleed
Till she died at the hands of her evil deed.
     Old Molly, Molly, Molly Means
     This is the ghost of Molly Means.

Sometimes at night through the shadowy trees
She rides along on a winter breeze.
You can hear her holler and whine and cry.
Her voice is thin and her moan is high,
And her cackling laugh or her barking cold
Bring terror to the young and old.
     O Molly, Molly, Molly Means
     Lean is the ghost of Molly Means.

October Journey / Margaret Walker

Traveller take heed for journeys undertaken in the dark of
    the year.
Go in the bright blaze of Autumn's equinox.
Carry protection against ravages of a sun-robber, a vandal,
    and a thief.
Cross no bright expanse of water in the full of the moon.
Choose no dangerous summer nights;
no heady tempting hours of spring;
October journeys are safest, brightest, and best.

I want to tell you what hills are like in October
when colors gush down mountainsides
and little streams are freighted with a caravan of leaves.
I want to tell you how they blush and turn in fiery shame and
    joy,
how their love burns with flames consuming and terrible
until we wake one morning and woods are like a smoldering
    plain—
a glowing caldron full of jewelled fire:
the emerald earth a dragon's eye
the poplars drenched with yellow light
and dogwoods blazing bloody red.

Travelling southward earth changes from gray rock to green
    velvet.
Earth changes to red clay
with green grass growing brightly
with saffron skies of evening setting dully
with muddy rivers moving sluggishly.

In the early spring when the peach tree blooms
wearing a veil like a lavender haze
and the pear and plum in their bridal hair
gently snow their petals on earth's grassy bosom below
then the soughing breeze is soothing

and the world seems bathed in tenderness,
but in October
blossoms have long since fallen.
A few red apples hang on leafless boughs;
wind whips bushes briskly.
And where a blue stream sings cautiously
a barren land feeds hungrily.

An evil moon bleeds drops of death.
The earth burns brown.
Grass shrivels and dries to a yellowish mass.
Earth wears a dun-colored dress
like an old woman wooing the sun to be her lover,
be her sweetheart and her husband bound in one.
Farmers heap hay in stacks and bind corn in shocks
against the biting breath of frost.

The train wheels hum, "I am going home, I am going home,
I am moving toward the South."
Soon cypress swamps and muskrat marshes
and black fields touched with cotton will appear.
I dream again of my childhood land
of a neighbor's yard with a redbud tree
the smell of pine for turpentine
an Easter dress, a Christmas eve
and winding roads from the top of a hill.
A music sings within my flesh
I feel the pulse within my throat
my heart fills up with hungry fear
while hills and flatlands stark and staring
before my dark eyes sad and haunting
appear and disappear.

Then when I touch this land again
the promise of a sun-lit hour dies.
The greenness of an apple seems
to dry and rot before my eyes.
The sullen winter rains
are tears of grief I cannot shed.

The windless days are static lives.
The clock runs down
timeless and still.
The days and nights turn hours to years
and water in a gutter marks the circle of another world
hating, resentful, and afraid
stagnant, and green, and full of slimy things.

The Fishes and the Poet's Hands / Frank Yerby

I

They say that when they burned young Shelley's corpse
(For he was drowned, you know, and washed ashore
With hands and face quite gone—the fishes had,
It seems, but small respect for Genius which
Came clothed in common flesh) the noise his brains
Made as they boiled and seethed within his skull
Could well be heard five yards away. At least
No one can hear *mine* as they boil; but then
He could not *feel* his burn; and so I think
He had the best of it at that. Don't you?

II

Now all the hungry broken men stand here
Beside my bed like ghosts and cry: "Why don't
You shout our wrongs aloud? Why are you not
Our voice, our sword? For you are of our blood;
You've seen us beaten, lynched, degraded, starved;
Men must be taught that other men are not
Mere pawns in some gigantic game in which
The winner takes the gold, the land, the work,

The breath, the heart, and soul of him who loses!"
I watch them standing there until my brain
Begins to burn within my head again—
(As Shelley's burned—poor, young dead Shelley whom
The fishes ate) then I get up and write
A very pretty sonnet, nicely rhymed
About my latest love affair, how sad
I am because some dear has thrown me for
A total loss. (But Shelley had me there.
All his affairs turned out quite well indeed;
Harriet in the river drowned for love
Of him; and Mary leaving Godwin's house
To follow where he led—quite well—indeed!)

III

You see, this is ironical and light
Because I am so sick, so hurt inside;
I'm tired of pretty rhyming words when all
The land where I was born is soaked in tears
And blood, and black and utter hopelessness.
Now I would make a new, strong, bitter song,
And hurl it in the teeth of those I hate—
I would stand tall and proud against their blows,
Knowing I could not win, I would go down
Grandly as an oak goes down, and leave
An echo of the crash, at least, behind.
(So Shelley lived—and so at last, he died.
The fishes ate his glorious hands; and all
That mighty bulk of brain boiled when they burned him!)

Weltschmerz / FRANK YERBY

For they who fashion songs must live too close to pain,
Acquaint themselves too well with grief and tears:
Must make the slow, deep, throbbing pulse of years
And their own heartbeats one; watch the slow train
Of passing autumns paint their scarlet stain
Upon the hills, and learn that beauty sears.
The whole world's woe and heartbreak must be theirs,
And theirs each vision smashed, each new dream slain.

But sing again, oh you who have the heart,
Sweet songs as fragile as a passing breath,
Although your broken heartstrings make your lyre,
And each pure strain must rend the soul apart;
For it was ever thus: to sing is death;
And in your spirit flames your body's pyre.

Wisdom / FRANK YERBY

I have known nights rain-washed and crystal-clear
And heavy with the mellow, mingled scent
Of honeysuckle, rose, and pine, while near
The shadowed ghosts of trees the new moon bent,
And touched your eyes with silvered ecstasy.

Then I believed in Magic, Youth, and Spring,
Then parting was synonymous with Death;
And every note I heard the night birds sing
Caused fitful haltings in my labored breath.

How strange that now I look into new eyes
In utter calm, yet with a deeper awe,
And know so well that when the old love dies
A new is born, as Spring from Winter's thaw
Arises in new light and loveliness.

And yet it is not quite the same to know
How transient grief, how fleeting, pain;
What prosaic love to stand and watch you go,
And, in a month, to be at peace again!

You Are a Part of Me / FRANK YERBY

You are a part of me. I do not know
By what slow chemistry you first became
A vital fiber of my being. Go
Beyond the rim of time or space, the same
Inflections of your voice will sing their way
Into the depths of my mind still. Your hair
Will gleam as bright, the artless play
Of word and glance, gesture and the fair
Young fingers waving, have too deeply etched
The pattern of your soul on mine. Forget
Me quickly as a laughing picture sketched
On water, I shall never know regret
Knowing no magic ever can set free
That part of you that is a part of me.

Calm After Storm / FRANK YERBY

Deep in my soul there roared the crashing thunder,
And unseen rain slashed furrows in my face;
The lightning's flame with tendrils fine as lace,
Etched intricate designs, too keen for wonder
Upon my dull-eyed soul. And that rich plunder
Of stolen joys, snatched in the little space,
Between the dawn and dark, had caught the pace,
This rip-tide of the heart, and was drawn under.

But this slow calm, this torpid lack of caring,
Creeping along, a drugged dream of content,
Kills no less surely than the storm's duress;
Better the winds, like thin whip-lashes sparing
No proud young heart until their force is spent,
Than this vague peace, akin to nothingness.

A Moment Please / SAMUEL ALLEN

When I gaze at the sun
    I walked to the subway booth
    for change for a dime.
and know that this great earth
    Two adolescent girls stood there
    alive with eagerness to know
is but a fragment from it thrown
    all in their new found world
    there was for them to know
in heat and flame a billion years ago,
    they looked at me and brightly asked
    "Are you Arabian?"

138

that then this world was lifeless
    I smiled and cautiously
    —for one grows cautious—
    shook my head.
as, a billion hence,
    "Egyptian?"
it shall again be,
    Again I smiled and shook my head
    and walked away.
what moment is it that I am betrayed,
    I've gone but seven paces now
oppressed, cast down,
    and from behind comes swift the sneer
or warm with love or triumph?
    "Or Nigger?"

    A moment, please
What is it that to fury I am roused?
    for still it takes a moment
What meaning for me
    and now
in this homeless clan
    I'll turn
the dupe of space
    and smile
the toy of time?
    and nod my head.

To Satch / Samuel Allen

Sometimes I feel like I will never stop
Just go forever
Till one fine morning
I'll reach up and grab me a handful of stars
And swing out my long lean leg
And whip three hot strikes burning down the heavens
And look over at God and say
How about that!

Here and Now / Catherine Cater

If here and now be but a timely span
Between today's unhappiness, tomorrow's
Joys, what if today's abundant sorrows
Never end, tomorrow never comes, what then?

If youth, impatient of the disrespect
Accorded it, yearns to be old,
Age chafes beneath the manifold
Losses of its prime and mourns neglect;

So let it be for here and now, my dear,
Not for the when of an eternity;
No gazer in the crystal ball can see
The future as we see the now and here.

Flags / Gwendolyn Brooks

Still, it is dear defiance now to carry
Fair flags of you above my indignation,
Top, with a pretty glory and a merry
Softness, the scattered pound of my cold passion.
I pull you down my foxhole. Do you mind?
You burn in bits of saucy color then.
I let you flutter out against the pained
Volleys. Against my power crumpled and wan.
You, and the yellow pert exuberance
Of dandelion days, unmocking sun;
The blowing of clear wind in your gay hair;
Love changeful in you (like a music, or
Like a sweet mournfulness, or like a dance,
Or like the tender struggle of a fan).

The Old-Marrieds / Gwendolyn Brooks

But in the crowding darkness not a word did they say.
Though the pretty-coated birds had piped so lightly all the
        day.
And he had seen the lovers in the little side streets.
And she had heard the morning stories clogged with sweets.
It was quite a time for loving. It was midnight. It was May.
But in the crowding darkness not a word did they say.

Piano After War / GWENDOLYN BROOKS

On a snug evening I shall watch her fingers,
Cleverly ringed, declining to clever pink,
Beg glory from the willing keys. Old hungers
Will break their coffins, rise to eat and thank.
And music, warily, like the golden rose
That sometimes after sunset warms the west,
Will warm that room, persuasively suffuse
That room and me, rejuvenate a past.
But suddenly, across my climbing fever
Of proud delight—a multiplying cry.
A cry of bitter dead men who will never
Attend a gentle maker of musical joy.
Then my thawed eye will go again to ice.
And stone will shove the softness from my face.

The Chicago *Defender* Sends a Man to Little Rock, Fall, 1957 / GWENDOLYN BROOKS

In Little Rock the people bear
Babes, and comb and part their hair
And watch the want ads, put repair
To roof and latch. While wheat toast burns
A woman waters multiferns.

Time upholds or overturns
The many, tight, and small concerns.

In Little Rock the people sing
Sunday hymns like anything,
Through Sunday pomp and polishing.

And after testament and tunes,
Some soften Sunday afternoons
With lemon tea and Lorna Doones.

I forecast
And I believe
Come Christmas Little Rock will cleave
To Christmas tree and trifle, weave,
From laugh and tinsel, texture fast.

In Little Rock is baseball; Barcarolle.
That hotness in July . . . the uniformed figures raw and
        implacable
And not intellectual,
Batting the hotness or clawing the suffering dust.
The Open Air Concert, on the special twilight green . . .
When Beethoven is brutal or whispers to ladylike air.
Blanket-sitters are solemn, as Johann troubles to lean
To tell them what to mean . . .
There is love, too, in Little Rock. Soft women softly
Opening themselves in kindness,
Or, pitying one's blindness,
Awaiting one's pleasure
In Azure
Glory with anguished rose at the root . . .
To wash away old semidiscomfitures.
They reteach purple and unsullen blue.
The wispy soils go. And uncertain
Half-havings have they clarified to sures.

In Little Rock they know
Not answering the telephone is a way of rejecting life,
That it is our business to be bothered, is our business
To cherish bores or boredom, be polite
To lies and love and many-faceted fuzziness.

I scratch my head, massage the hate-I-had.
I blink across my prim and pencilled pad.
The saga I was sent for is not down.
Because there is a puzzle in this town.

The biggest News I do not dare
Telegraph to the Editor's chair:
"They are like people everywhere."
The angry Editor would reply
In hundred harryings of Why.

And true, they are hurling spittle, rock,
Garbage and fruit in Little Rock.
And I saw coiling storm a-writhe
On bright madonnas. And a scythe
Of men harassing brownish girls.
(The bows and barrettes in the curls
And braids declined away from joy.)

I saw a bleeding brownish boy . . .
The lariat lynch-wish I deplored.
The loveliest lynchee was our Lord.

The African Affair / BRUCE McM. WRIGHT

Black is what the prisons are,
The stagnant vortex of the hours
Swept into totality,
Creeping in the perjured heart,
Bitter in the vulgar rhyme,
Bitter on the walls;

Black is where the devils dance
With time within
The creviced wall. Time pirouettes
A crippled orbit in a trance,
And crawls below, beneath the flesh
Where darkness flows;

Black is where the deserts burn,
The Niger and Sasandra flow,
From where the Middle Passage went
Within the Continent of Night
From Cameroons to Carisbrooke
And places conscience cannot go;

Black is where thatched temples burn
Incense to carved ebon-wood;
Where traders shaped my father's pain,
His person and his place,
Among dead statues in a frieze,
In the spectrum of his race.

Sonnet / ALFRED A. DUCKETT

Where are we to go when this is done?
Will we slip into old, accustomed ways,
finding remembered notches, one by one?
Thrashing a hapless way through quickening haze?

Who is to know us when the end has come?
Old friends and families, but could we be
strange to the sight and stricken dumb
at visions of some pulsing memory?

Who will love us for what we used to be
who now are what we are, bitter or cold?
Who is to nurse us with swift subtlety
back to the warm and feeling human fold?

Where are we to go when this is through?
We are the war-born. What are we to do?

Sunset Horn / MYRON O'HIGGINS

*Enduring peace is the only monument civilization can raise
to the millions who have perished in its cause.*

I

Block the cannon; let no trumpets sound!
Our power is manifest in other glory;
Our flesh in this contested slope of ground.

In thin silences we lie, pale strangers to the corn-gold
      morning,
Repeating what the fathers told . . . the promised legacy
      of tall sons:
The hushed sibilants of peace; and the far tomorrow on the
      hills.

O we went quickly or a little longer
And for a space saw caste and categories, creeds and race
Evaporate into the flue of common circumstance.
We sought transcendent meaning for our struggle,
And in that rocking hour, each minute, each narrow second
Fell upon us like a rain of knives.
We grappled here an instant, then singly, or in twos or tens,
      or by bewildered hundreds,
Were pulverized . . . Reduced . . . Wiped out—
Made uniform and equal!
                And let us tell you this:
Death is indiscriminate . . . and easier . . . than sorrow,
      fear, or fallen pride.
There is no road back. We rest in ultimates;
In calmness come abrupt by bomb, or bullet, or abbreviated
      dream;
With conflicts spent.
This stark convergent truth continues,
Linking us through slim unseen dimensions—we to you, we
      to you . . .

II

While you cry Victory! or Surrender!
Turn these figures in the head,
Clean impersonal round numbers,
Ordered inventory of the dead.

Regard these slender nines and ones;
These trailing threes and fives; these fours and sevens, bent
    and angular;
Delicately drawn, divided into ranks by commas,
Staggered down the page in regimented squads and columns:
These are our mute effigies, trim and shining,
Passing in review . . .

                O Drummer, obediently we come,
Down through the assassin's street,
The company of death in splendid array! . . .

But leave us to the terrible fields.
Yours is the pomp of brasses, the counterfeit peace, the
    dynasty of lies . . .
We are but dabs of flesh blown to the cliffs,
Or ragged stumps of legs that moved too slowly toward the
    brush.
And our song: we joined no swelling harmony of voices.
Those final incoherent sounds we made;
Those startled oaths that bubbled through the blood bogged
    in our throats;
That last falsetto cry of terror;
Were a jagged threnody, swallowed whole and drowned in
    cacophonic floods.
This was our sunset horn . . .

Let these be added with the spoils for quick division!
Set these down in sharp italics on the page
For scholars' documents!

III

Raise no vain monuments; bury us down!
Our power is manifest in other glory;

Our flesh in this contested slope of ground.
There is no more but these, a legacy, a grim prediction . . .
Let the scent and sounds of death go limp
And flounder in the valleys and the streets.
And for those crafty ones—those who speak our names in
      brief professional remembrance
To garner votes and profits, or practice quick extortion—
Let other music find their ears.
And give them for a souvenir this clown's disguise
Of swastikas and Roman standards, of scythes and suns and
      dollar signs . . .
One day the rest of you will know the meaning of annihilation.
And the hills will rock with voltage;
And the forests burn like a flaming broom;
And the stars explode and drop like cinders on the land.
And these steel cities where no love is—
You shall see them fall and vanish in a thunder of erupting
      suns!

O you shall know; and in that day, traveler, O in that day
When the tongues confound, and breath is total in the horn,
Your Judas eyes, seeking truth at last, will search for us
And borrow ransom from this bowel of violence!

And on This Shore / M. CARL HOLMAN

Alarm and time clock still intrude too early,
Sun on the lawns at morning is the same,
Across the cups we yawn at private murders,
Accustomed causes leave us gay or glum.

(I feel the streaming wind in my eyes,
the highway swimming under the floor,
music flung comically over the hills,

148

Remember your profile, your pilot's body at ease,
the absolute absence of boredom, the absence of fear)

The swingshift workers are snoring at noon,
The army wife's offspring dumb in his crib,
The private, patron of blackmarket still,
Sleeps long past reveille stark on his slab.

(The chimes were musing far beyond soft hills,
I brushed an ant from your arm,
The leaves lifted, shifted like breathing to pour
Light on your lids, seemed then no end of time)

The streets rewind to spools of home,
Dials usher in the bland newscaster,
From the mailbox's narrow room
Lunges the cobra of disaster.

(Kissed and were happy at the door,
showered, pretending this would last,
Stones down dead wells, the calendar
counts summers that are lost, are lost)

II

Is it yourself he loves
Or the way you arranged your hair?
The book which taught you to listen while he talked?
The cute dance steps and that night on the Navy pier?
Did he see yours or another's face when he waked?
On what does this shadow feed
And shall it not fade?

Is it yourself she loves
Or the easy-come money you breezily spend?
The 4-F, convertible, "A" coupons, dark market Scotch?
Would she stick if she found she could interest your friend:
When the man on her dresser returns will you prove his
        match?
On what does this shadow feed
And shall it not fade?

Is it yourself they love
Or the victories panted with vibrant voice?
(Mellow for brave boys sleeping their last long sleep)
Will sponsor and fan abide when bulletins burst in your face,
Raw stumps and barricade explode through the map?
On what does this shadow feed,
And shall it not fade?

Is it yourself they love,
You brief-cased and lens-familiar,
Invoking spring from the smoke of our heaviest winter?
Their mouths adore—but fangs may lurk for anger;
Watching night wither do you not sometimes wonder
On what does this shadow feed
And shall it not fade?

Letter Across Doubt and Distance / M. CARL HOLMAN

I dreamed all my fortitude screamed
And fled down the strict corridor,
Entered in greedy and unashamed
At the seductive door;
Or your eyes winked from the tabloid,
Your silence raised a wraith
Which lured me nearer that void
Where fact prepares its ambuscade for faith.

Carved keen in the spring-green bark
Your long absence does not congeal,
No cement sutures the cruel crack
Where the hot sap weeps still
And will furrow and blister this sand
Though vanes claim weather is north

Until your gifted hand
Heals the shocked tissues and late buds flame forth:

O girl waking now where the swirl
Of gulls scatters across white hulls
And the wind hurtling the marshy field
Spurs the green bay into hills,
All my pain falls at your power,
Slacks and comes softly to rest.
Calmed, as that gray church tower
Checks the wild pigeons taking them to breast.

Notes for a Movie Script / M. CARL HOLMAN

Fade in the sound of summer music,
Picture a hand plunging through her hair,
Next his socked feet and her scuffed dance slippers
Close, as they kiss on the rug-stripped stair.

Catch now the taxi from the station,
Capture her shoulders' sudden sag;
Switch to him silent in the barracks
While the room roars at the corporal's gag.

Let the drums dwindle in the distance,
Pile the green sea above the land;
While she prepares a single breakfast,
Reading the V mail in her hand.

Ride a cold moonbeam to the pillbox,
Sidle the camera to his feet
Sprawled just outside in the gummy grasses,
Swollen like nightmare and not neat.

Now doorbell nudges the lazy morning:
She stills the sweeper for a while,
Twitches her dress, swings the screendoor open,
Cut—with no music—on her smile.

Song / M. Carl Holman

Dressed up in my melancholy
With no place to go,
Sick as sin of inwardness
And sick of being so

I walked out on the avenue,
Eager to give my hand
To any with the health to heal
Or heart to understand.

I had not walked a city block
And met with more than ten
Before I read the testament
Stark behind each grin:

Beneath the hatbrims haunting me,
More faithful than a mirror,
The figuration of my grief,
The image of my error.

Christmas Lullaby for a New-Born Child / Yvonne Gregory

"Where did I come from, Mother, and why?"
"You slipped from the hand of Morn.
A child's clear eyes have wondered why
Since the very first child was born."

"What shall I do here, Mother, and when?"
"You'll dream in a waking sleep,
Then sow your dreams in the minds of men
Till the time shall come to reap."

"What do men long for, Mother, and why?"
"They long for a star's bright rays,
And when they have glimpsed a tiny light
They follow with songs of praise."

"Where does that star shine, Mother, and when?"
"It glows in the hearts of a few.
So close your eyes, while I pray, dear child,
That the star may shine in you."

Far From Africa: Four Poems / Margaret Danner

"are you beautiful still?"

1. GARNISHING THE AVIARY

Our moulting days are in their twilight stage.
These lengthy dreaded suns of draggling plumes.
These days of moods that swiftly alternate between

The former preen (ludicrous now) and a downcast rage
Or crestfallen lag, are fading out. The initial bloom;
Exotic, dazzling in its indigo, tangerine

Splendor; this rare, conflicting coat had to be shed.
Our drooping feathers turn all shades. We spew
This unamicable aviary, gag upon the worm, and fling

Our loosening quills. We make a riotous spread
Upon the dust and mire that beds us. We do not shoo
So quickly; but the shades of the pinfeathers resulting

From this chaotic push, though still exotic,
Blend in more easily with those on the wings
Of the birds surrounding them; garnishing
The aviary, burnishing this zoo.

2. DANCE OF THE ABAKWETA

Imagine what Mrs. Haessler would say
If she could see the Watusi youth dance
Their well-versed initiation. At first glance
As they bend to an invisible barre
You would know that she had designed their costumes.

For though they were made of pale beige bamboo straw
Their lines were the classic tutu. Nothing varied.
Each was cut short at the thigh and carried
High to a degree of right angles. Nor was there a flaw
In their leotards. Made of leopard skin or the hide

Of a goat, or the Gauguin-colored Okapi's striped coat
They were cut in her reverenced "tradition."
She would have approved their costumes and positions.
And since neither Iceland nor Africa is too remote
For her vision she would have wanted to form

A "traditional" ballet. Swan Lake, Scheherazade or
(After seeing their incredible leaps)
Les Orientales. Imagine the exotic sweep
Of such a ballet, and from the way the music pours

Over these dancers (this tinkling of bells, talking
Of drums, and twanging of tan, sandalwood harps)
From this incomparable music, Mrs. Haessler of Vassar can
Glimpse strains of Tchaikovsky, Chopin
To accompany her undeviatingly sharp
"Traditional" ballet. I am certain that if she could
Tutor these potential protégés, as
Quick as Aladdin rubbing his lamp, she would.

3. THE VISIT OF THE PROFESSOR OF AESTHETICS

To see you standing in the sagging bookstore door
So filled me with chagrin that suddenly you seemed as
Pink and white to me as a newborn, hairless mouse. For

I had hoped to delight you at home. Be a furl
Of faint perfume and Vienna's cordlike lace.
To shine my piano till a shimmer of mother-of-pearl

Embraced it. To pleasantly surprise you with the grace
That transcends my imitation and much worn
"Louis XV" couch. To display my Cathedrals and ballets.

To plunge you into Africa through my nude
Zulu Prince, my carvings from Benin, forlorn
Treasures garnered by much sacrifice of food.

I had hoped to delight you, for more
Rare than the seven-year bloom of my
Chinese spiderweb fern is a mind like yours

That concedes my fetish for this substance
Of your trade. And I had planned to prove
Your views of me correct at even every chance

Encounter. But you surprised me. And the store which
Had shown promise until you came, arose
Like a child gone wild when company comes or a witch

At Hallowe'en. The floor, just swept and mopped,
Was persuaded by the northlight to deny it.
The muddy rag floor rugs hunched and flopped

Away from the tears in the linoleum that I wanted
Them to hide. The drapes that I had pleated
In clear orchid and peach feverishly flaunted

Their greasiest folds like a banner.
The books who had been my friends, retreated—
Became as shy as the proverbial poet in manner

And hid their better selves. All glow had been deleted
By the dirt. And I felt that you whose god is grace
Could find no semblance of it here. And unaware

That you were scrubbing, you scrubbed your hands.
Wrung and scrubbed your long white fingers. Scrubbed
Them as you smiled and I lowered my eyes from despair.

4. ETTA MOTEN'S ATTIC

(Filled with mementos of African journeys)

It was as if Gauguin
had upset a huge paint pot
of his incomparable tangerine,

splashing wherever my startled eyes ran
here and there, and at my very hand on
masques and paintings and carvings not seen

here before, spilling straight as a stripe
spun geometrically in a Nbeble rug
flung over an ebony chair,

or dripping round as a band on a type
of bun the Watusi warriors
make of their pompadoured hair,

splashing high as a sunbird or fly moving
over a frieze of mahogany trees,
or splotching out from low underneath as a root,

shimmering bright as a ladybug grooving
a green bed of moss, sparkling as a beetle,
a bee, shockingly dotting the snoot

of an ape or the nape of its neck or as clue
to its navel, stamping a Zulu's
intriguing masque, tipping

the lips of a chief of Ashantis who
was carved to his stool so he'd sit
there forever and never fear a slipping

of rule or command, dyeing the skirt
(all askew) that wouldn't stay put on the
Pygmy in spite of his real leather belt,

quickening and charming till we felt the bloom
of veldt and jungle flow through the room.

The Slave and the Iron Lace / MARGARET DANNER

The craving of Samuel Rouse for clearance to create
was surely as hot as the iron that buffeted him. His passion
for freedom so strong that it molded the smouldering
            fashions
he laced, for how else could a slave plot
or counterplot such incomparable shapes,

form or reform, for house after house
the intricate Chatilion Patio pattern, the delicate
Rose and Lyre, the Debutante Settee
the complex but famous Grape; frame the classic vein
in an iron bench?

How could he turn an iron Venetian urn, wind the Grape
            Vine chain
the trunk of a pine with a Round-the-Tree-settee,
mold a Floating Flower tray, a French chair, create all this
in such exquisite fairyland taste, that he'd be freed
and his skill would still resound a hundred years after?

And I wonder if I, with this thick asbestos glove of an
attitude, could lace, forge, and bend this ton of lead-chained
     spleen

surrounding me?
Could I manifest and sustain it into a new free-form screen
of, not necessarily love, but (at the very least,
for all concerned) grace.

A Private Letter to Brazil / G. C. ODEN

The map shows me where it is you are. I
am here, where the words NEW YORK run an inch
out to sea, ending where GULF STREAM flows by.

The coastline bristles with place names. The pinch
in printing space has launched them offshore
with the fishbone's fine-tooth spread, to clinch

their urban identity. Much more
noticeable it is in the chain
of hopscotching islands that, loosely, moors

your continent to mine. (Already plain
is its eastward drift, and who could say
what would become of it left free!) Again,

the needle-pine alignment round S/A,
while where it is you are (or often go),
RIO, spills its subtle phonic bouquet

farthest seawards of all. Out there I know
the sounding is some deep 2000 feet,
and the nationalized current tours so

pregnant with resacas. In their flux meets
all the subtlety of God's great nature
and man's terse grief. See, Hero, at your feet

is not that slight tossing dead Leander?

The Carousel / G. C. ODEN

*"I turned from side to side, from image to image to put you
down."*—Louise Bogan

An empty carousel in a deserted park
rides me round and round,
forth and back,
from end to beginning,
like the tail that drives the dog.

I cannot see:
sight focusses shadow where once
pleased scenery,
and in this whirl of space
only the indefinite is constant.

This is the way of grief:
spinning in the rhythm of memories
that will not let you up
or down,
but keeps you grinding through
a granite air.

". . . As When Emotion Too Far Exceeds Its Cause"
—Elizabeth Bishop / G. C. ODEN

You probably could put their names to them.
The birds, I mean.
Though I have often watched their rushing
about the upper air
(deliberate as subway riders
who are not anywhere near
so orderly),
I have never stopped to inquire the name
of that one or another.
Still, I did take time
to observe them in their dips and circles
and jet-propelled ascendancies.

It's all in the wings I am told.
That could be said of angels.
I grant it may be true;
undoubtedly is,
since my informants know more
than I. But,
still, I wonder,
and harbor fear that we all are wrong
to think that birds do fly.
What if, one day, upon the ground with us
we found them;
their wings unable to lift them
anywhere except into a deeper stratum
of despair.
Would it all be a matter of wings?
Does flight depend upon such feathered things?

Or is it air? I do not trust the stuff.
Seeing the birds beating about in it,
I want to say, "Take care; and
don't believe in what it seems you do!"
Sometimes I stray across a small one

I should have said it to;
one who for all his modern design
to sweep and arch the atmosphere
had plummeted, instead, to earth
and worms that do not care about horizons.
If I retreat,
too shocked to cast the benediction
of a single leaf,
understand why:
I know the error in invisible support;
in love's celestial venturing
I, too, once trusted air
that plunged me down.
Yes, I!

The Map / G. C. ODEN

My rug is red. My couch, whereon I deal
in dreams with truths I never live, is brown;
a shading more intense than that by my
skin declared. Richer it is, too, than of
any of the eight clear hues coloring
my wide, world map soldiering the white wall
there behind it. This map is of the world.
It says so. In type ½″ high: WORLD;
and with what I know of maps I do, in
deed, believe it—though over it, in type
now smaller by one-half, I read the word
"COSMOPOLITAN," and over that, in
type yet smaller by one-half, these gentile
modifiers "RAND McNALLY."

                              The seas
square off in blue. Or, ought the word be "sea?"
Uniformly bright, planed by a tone so
mild you might suppose the North Sea twinned the
South and that the Moskenstraumen was (for
the most part) Poe (quote) SAILING DIRECTIONS
FOR THE NORTHWEST AND NORTH COAST OF
      NORWAY
(unquote) to the contrary; seven diminishes
to one, where none arrests attention.

                                          Not
so the land. Flowering forth as spring in
May will settle down to deed, it woos us
with such yellows, pinks and greens as would, I'm
sure, lure the most selective butterfly;
and each trim hue is sized the living room
of nations.

                    America (U. S.) is
daffodil; Canada carnation; while
leaflike as an elephant ear, Greenland
hangs indifferent to those arctic winds parching
the cell-like bounds of Russia (here halved and
showing both to the left and right of this
our hemisphere—indeed, as is a good
part of the orient split, some even
to doubling appearance.)

                              Europe (also)
lies fragmented; though from nature's—not the
mapmaker's—division. Ireland off-
set from England, offset from France (feigning
oasis besides the rot-brown fill to
Germany) supplies one awkward revel
of abstraction as that gross bud of Spain
(with Portugal) patterns another; not
to mention Italy's invasion of
the sea.

                                                        162

Norway, Sweden, much as giraffes
must bend, towards Denmark group in restricted
covenant; yet, though this canvas—Europe—
at its center holds, such unity rests
more upon imagination than that,
let's say, of Africa islanded in
those deeper latitudes.

There, it is the
green (again) I think. Incandescent flood
like the dead reckoning of spring; at four
points edging sea; it seems a fever of
the mind within that broad head housed (it shapes
—Africa—a head to me!) which in its
course will blaze the length of continent as
now it fires breadth.

And who will say it
won't? Not the mapmaker, surely, who must
exact truth. Not I, high hoisting same to,
state whirlwind. Will you, because you might not
particularly care to see it so?

The Rebel / MARI E. EVANS

When I
die
I'm sure
I will have a
Big Funeral . . .
Curiosity
seekers . . .
coming to see

if I
am really
Dead . . .
or just
trying to make
Trouble. . . .

When in Rome / Mari E. Evans

Marrie dear
the box is full . . .
take
whatever you like
to eat . . .

       (an egg
       or soup
       . . . there ain't no meat.)

there's endive there
and
cottage cheese . . .

      (whew! if I had some
      black-eyed peas . . .)

there's sardines
on the shelves
and such . . .
but
don't
get my anchovies . . .

they cost
too much!

>   (me get the
>   anchovies indeed!
>   what she think, she got—
>   a bird to feed?)

there's plenty in there
to fill you up . . .

>   (yes'm. just the
>   sight's
>   enough!

>   Hope I lives till I get
>   home
>   I'm tired of eatin'
>   what they eats in Rome . . .)

The Emancipation of George-Hector
(a colored turtle) / MARI E. EVANS

George-Hector
. . . is
spoiled.
formerly he stayed
well up in his
shell . . . but now
he hangs arms and legs
sprawlingly
in a most languorous fashion . . .
head rared back
to

be
admired.

he didn't use to
talk . . .
but
he does now.

Raison d'Etre / OLIVER PITCHER

Over the eye behind the moon's cloud
over you whose touch to a Stradavari heart shames
the chorale of angels
over Mr. Eros who tramples the sun-roses
and sits amid willow trees
to weep
over the olive wood
over the vibrant reds, blacks, luminous golds of
decay
over the strength of silence and advantages of
unwareness
over the Rosey Eclipse
over the geyser in the toilet bowl
over the cynical comma
over the madness itself
the occupational hazard of artists
over the catcher caught in his catcher's mitt
over oil and opal, blood and bone of
the earth
over the iron touch behind pink gloves
over retired civilizations sunken below levels
shimmering in rusty lustre
over myself
I wave the flag raison d'etre

Four Questions Addressed to His Excellency, the Prime Minister / JAMES P. VAUGHN

Sir

I read of late
you have tired of roses
their habit of unfolding
a beginning middle and end

The stenographer unbuttons her blouse
spring rains
porcelain is everywhere

On a ledge
high above the stunned constituency
the cabinet sits
in cold tuxedos

Sir

Is it true
that when the idea is cut out
there is profuse bleeding
in the mind

around her gilded neck
Madame la Femme
Winds and winds
her silken drama

tassels wrestle
together
create a slight colloquial rhyme

Sir

if labor agrees
and management agrees
where does the grammarian
put the prefix

however nimble
skulduggery
the electorate stands pat
and opposition of weights
is felt

Shhh

Madeline is entering
her tomb appears surprised
sit sit

Sir

according to one historian
snow is a visual cadenza
remember

swiftly the skier passes
deeper and deeper into silence
the telephone rings
hello hello hello

the caretaker
boards the windows of the summer cottage
the lord chamberlain shivers
a moment sped by

So? / JAMES P. VAUGHN

Nothing if not utterly in death
   So let us now demur flowers
   Say you saw us in patience
   Gently remove wrath from thorn
   And nod "Morning" to moon passing

Happy if merely knowing light
I cannot grasp substances, but
If by chance, I drop my world
And hear it smash in the basin
I rejoice in the sound, if not fancy.

Let it stand at that. If with
These eyes I encourage the
Great Distances to move closer
And sit here with me in silence
Then will such bright candles as these
Be not held hostages too soon.

At War / RUSSELL ATKINS

Beyond the turning sea's far foam
a tender ephemera
of a moment's dawn in a fantastic place
sudden'd its appear
and was gone!

was gone
out, as a young man farewell'd to all
            but arms!

don't ask me more
what of it, of it why
I cannot explain it any—
no don't ask me, I insist—
some dared and
died—

Listen a moment—! Sh! Listen—!
that hurrying as of a shore of
fugitives!

Irritable Song / RUSSELL ATKINS

Says-so is in a woe of shuddered
    leaves
Foreboding huskily.
For who returns (said by its rasp)
Save leniently chanced
To the begun? There is fatal
    instance.

A low hanging of bough
Plucked my eye; automobile
Wheels, furious by,
Stuck objects upon
Of a deadly bruise
And strew the stone;

A footfall behind'll
Be the gunman's I swear.
None the worse when I
Am in the hearse.
Should I return, the house
(What less?) is gone:
Burned into none.

Or say upon return
Coronary farewell
Leaves me lie. Ugh!
Dare, sir? Be nay'd
Tomorrow, tomorrow
    in today?

It's Here In The / Russell Atkins

Here in the newspaper—the wreck of the East Bound.
A photograph bound to bring on cardiac asthenia.
There is a blur that mists the page!
On one side is a gloom of dreadful harsh.
Then breaks flash lights up sheer.
There is much huge about. I suppose then
            those no's are people
        between that suffering of—
        (what more have we? for Christ's sake, no!)
Something of a full stop of it
crash of blood and the still shock
        of stark sticks and an immense swift gloss,
And two dead no's lie aghast still.
One casts a crazed eye and the other's
Closed dull.
            the heap up twists
                such
as to harden the unhard and unhard
the hardened.

Lester Young / Ted Joans

Sometimes he was cool like an eternal
        blue flame burning in the old Kansas
        City nunnery
Sometimes he was happy 'til he'd think
        about his birth place and its blood
        stained clay hills and crow-filled trees

Most times he was blowin' on the wonderful
    tenor sax of his, preachin' in very cool
    tones, shouting only to remind you of
    a certain point in his blue messages
He was our president as well as the minister
    of soul stirring Jazz, he knew what he
    blew, and he did what a prez should do,
    wail, wail, wail. There were many of
    them to follow him and most of them were
    fair—but they never spoke so eloquently
    in so a far out funky air.
Our prez done died, he know'd this would come
    but death has only booked him, alongside
    Bird, Art Tatum, and other heavenly wailers.
Angels of Jazz—they don't die—they live
they live—in hipsters like you and I

Voice in the Crowd / TED JOANS

If you should see/a man/walking
    down a crowded street/ talking aloud/ to himself
    don't run/in the opposite direction
        but run toward him/for he is a *poet!*

    You have nothing to fear/from the poet
    but the truth

Harlem Sounds: Hallelujah Corner / WILLIAM BROWNE

Cymbals clash,
and in this scene
of annulled jazz,
gay-stepping stompers
roll in
shouting 'Hallelujah'
at a deposed 'Spirit'
until,
like a mimic-child,
it rages,
stumbles,
and lies exhausted,
strung like Jesus.

The honky-tonk
riffs,
runs,
and breaks,
are superimposed
on the sounds
of
weeping
amens.

The mandrill sounds
of tuba snorts,
coned by applauding tambourines;
laugh
at the banjo-dance
of amen-women
shouting
at the
boogie-woogie
voice
of God.

The Voyage of Jimmy Poo / JAMES A. EMANUEL

A soapship went a-rocking
Upon a bathtub sea.
The sailor crouched a-smiling
Upon a dimpled knee.

Young Neptune dashed the waters
Against enamel shore,
And kept the air a-tumbling
With bubble-clouds galore.

But soon the voyage ended.
The ship was swept away
By a hand that seemed to whisper
"There'll be no more games today."

The ship lay dry and stranded
On a shiny metal tray,
And a voice was giving orders
That a sailor must obey.

Oh captain, little captain,
Make room for just one more
The next time you go sailing
Beyond enamel shore.

The Treehouse / JAMES A. EMANUEL

To every man
His treehouse,
A green splice in the humping years,

Spartan with narrow cot
And prickly door.

To every man
His twilight flash
Of luminous recall

    of tiptoe years
    in leaf-stung flight;
    of days of squirm and bite
    that waved antennas through the grass;
    of nights
    when every moving thing
    was girlshaped,
    expectantly turning.

To every man
His house below
And his house above—
With perilous stairs
Between.

Get Up, Blues / JAMES A. EMANUEL

Blues
Never climb a hill
Or sit on a roof
In starlight.

Blues
Just bend low
And moan in the street
And shake a borrowed cup.

Blues
Just sit around
Sipping,
Hatching yesterdays.

Get up, Blues.
Fly.
Learn what it means
To be up high.

Four Sheets to the Wind and a One-Way Ticket to France, 1933 / CONRAD KENT RIVERS

As a Black Child I was a dreamer
I bought a red scarf and women told me how
Beautiful it looked.
Wandering through the heart of France
As France wandered through me.

In the evenings,
I would watch the funny people make love,
My youth allowed me the opportunity to hear
All those strange
Verbs conjugated in erotic affirmations,
I knew love at twelve.

When Selassie went before his peers and
Africa gained dignity
I read in two languages, not really caring
Which one belonged to me.

My mother lit a candle for King George,
My father went broke, we died.
When I felt blue, the champs understood,

And when it was crowded, the alley
Behind Harry's New York bar soothed my
Restless spirit.

I liked to watch the Bohemians gaze at the
Paintings along Gauguin's bewildered paradise.

Bracque once passed me in front of the Café Musique
I used to watch those sneaky professors examine
The populace,
American never quite fitted in, but they
Tried, so we smiled.

I guess the money was too much for my folks,
Hitler was such a prig and a scare, they caught
The last boat.
    I stayed.

Main street was never the same, I read Gide
And tried to
Translate Proust. (Now nothing is real except
French wine.)
For absurdity is reality, my loneliness unreal,

And I shall die an old Parisian, with much honor.

To Richard Wright / CONRAD KENT RIVERS

You said that your people
Never knew the full spirit of
Western Civilization.
To be born unnoticed
Is to be born black,
And left out of the grand adventure.

Miseducation, denial,
Are lost in the cruelty of oppression.
And the faint cool kiss of sensuality
Lingers on our cheeks.

The quiet terror brings on silent night.
They are driving us crazy. And our father's
Religion warps his life.

To live day by day
   Is not to live at all.

Preface to a Twenty Volume Suicide Note
LeRoi Jones
(For Kellie Jones, born 16 May 1959)

Lately, I've become accustomed to the way
The ground opens up and envelops me
Each time I go out to walk the dog.
Or the broad-edged silly music the wind
Makes when I run for a bus . . .

Things have come to that.

And now, each night I count the stars,
And each night I get the same number.
And when they will not come to be counted,
I count the holes they leave.

Nobody sings anymore.

And then last night, I tiptoed up
To my daughter's room and heard her
Talking to someone, and when I opened

The door, there was no one there . . .
Only she on her knees, peeking into

Her own clasped hands.

The Invention of Comics / LeRoi Jones

I am a soul in the world: in
the world of my soul the whirled
light from the day
the sacked land
of my father.

In the world, the sad
nature of
myself. In myself
nature is sad. Small
prints of the day. Its
small dull fires. Its
sun, like a greyness
smeared on the dark.

The day of my soul, is
the nature of that
place. It is a landscape. Seen
from the top of a hill. A
grey expanse; dull fires
throbbing on its seas.

The man's soul, the complexion
of his life. The menace
of its greyness. The
fire, throbs, the sea
moves. Birds shoot

from the dark. The edge
of the waters lit
darkly for the moon.

And the moon, from the soul. Is
the world, of the man. The man
and his sea, and its moon, and
the soft fire throbbing. Kind
death. O
my dark and sultry
love.

As a Possible Lover / LeRoi Jones

Practices
silence, the way of wind
bursting
its early lull. Cold morning
to night, we go so
slowly, without
thought
to ourselves. (Enough
to have thought
tonight, nothing
finishes it. What
you are, will have
no certainty, or
end. That you will
stay, where you are,
a human gentle wisp
of life. Ah . . .)
       practices

loneliness,
as a virtue. A single
specious need
to keep
what you have
never really
had.

The End of Man Is His Beauty / LeRoi Jones

And silence
which proves but
a referent
to my disorder.
            Your world shakes

cities die
beneath your shape.
            The single shadow

at noon
like a live tree
whose leaves
are like clouds

weightless soul
at whose love faith moves
as a dark and
withered day.

They speak of singing who
have never heard song; of living
whose deaths are legends
for their kind.

A scream
gathered in wet fingers
at the top of its stalk.
—They have passed
and gone
whom you thought your lovers

In this perfect quiet, my friend,
their shapes
are not unlike
night's

Celebrated Return / CLARENCE MAJOR

1. a circus of battleships carrying heavy laughter passes be-
neath a bridge which may be lifted and each has been as-
signed a draft and thus lifted but those laughing were ficti-
tious representatives of the human race no matter how more
harmonious they were they had just left the land where
dromedaries are plenty and men go in droll groups in robes
with beards but their laughter was an excavated kind of shel-
ter from the dubious plight of anger.

2. ashore gawky measures of folk of the nature of insubstan-
tiality waited in dull booming upon the science of the earth
for the circus of mirth which now pushed the waves forward
as the battleships of embellishment encircled the geometry
of the solid sunstruck people shouting now at last.
   Gloria in Excelsis
   Gloria in Excelsis
   Gloria in Excelsis
      Gloria Patri
      Gloria Patri
      Gloria Patri

No Time for Poetry / Julia Fields

Midnight is no time for
Poetry—
   The heart is much too
calm
   The spirit too lagging
   and dull—
But the morning!
With the sunshine in one's eyes
and breath—
And all the pink clouds
Like chiffon in a dressing gown
And the orange-white mists
That leap and furl—

Ah, I should greet the morning
   As though I never saw a morning before
And only heard that it
   was this or that,
Gossip that was good either way,
There being nothing derogatory to say.

And in that strange-white mist
I'd be content to go upon the paths
with neither shoes nor hat
winding my way away from home
much like a
   cornerless cat
Holding vibrations of laughter in my
Fur
   That floated from who knows where
   and goes who-less-could-care.

There are no orange-white mists
   at midnight
   They are a world away
   And so
   Midnight is not time for Poetry

The Bishop of Atlanta: Ray Charles /
HORACE JULIAN BOND

The Bishop seduces the world with his voice
Sweat strangles mute eyes
As insinuations gush out through a hydrant of sorrow
Dreams, a world never seen
Moulded on Africa's anvil, tempered down home
Documented in cries and wails
Screaming to be ignored, crooning to be heard
Throbbing from the gutter
On Saturday night
Silver offering only
The Right Reverend's back in town
Don't it make you feel all right?

Two Jazz Poems / CARL WENDELL HINES, JR.

#

yeah here am i
am standing
at the crest of a tallest
hill with a trumpet
in my hand & dark
glasses
on.
    bearded & bereted i proudly stand!
      but there are no eyes to see me.
    i send down cool sounds!
      but there are no ears to hear me.

my lips they quiver in aether-emptiness!
     there are no hearts to love me.
surely though through night's grey fog mist
of delusion & dream
& the rivers of tears that flow
like gelatin soul-juice
some apathetic bearer of
paranoidic peyote visions (or some
other source of inspiration) shall
     hear the song i play. shall
     see the beard & beret. shall
     become inflamed beyond all hope
with emotion's everlasting fire
& join me
     in
          eternal
                    Peace.
& but yet well
who knows?

          #

there he stands. see?
like a black Ancient Mariner his
wrinkled old face so
full of the wearies of living is
turned downward with
closed eyes. his frayed-collar
faded-blue old shirt turns
dark with sweat & the old
necktie undone drops
loosely about the worn
old jacket see? just
barely holding his
sagging stomach in. yeah.
his run-down shoes have
paper in them & his
rough unshaven face shows

pain
in each wrinkle.

but there he stands. in
self-brought solitude head
still down eyes
still closed ears
perked & trained upon
the bass line for
across his chest lies an old
alto saxophone—
supported from his neck by
a wire coat hanger.

gently he lifts it now
to parted lips. see? to
tell all the world that
he is a Black Man. that
he was sent here to preach
the Black Gospel of Jazz.

now preaching it with words of
screaming notes & chords he
is no longer a man. no not even
a Black Man. but (yeah!)
a Bird!—
one that gathers his wings & flies
   high
      high
         higher
until he flies away! or
comes back to find himself
a Black Man
again.

Cocoa Morning / BOB KAUFMAN

Variations on a theme by morning,
Two lady birds move in the distance.
Gray jail looming, bathed in sunlight.
Violin tongues whispering.

Drummer, hummer, on the floor,
Dreaming of wild beats, softer still,
Yet free of violent city noise,
Please, sweet morning,
Stay here forever.

I Have Folded My Sorrows / BOB KAUFMAN

I have folded my sorrows into the mantle of summer night,
Assigning each brief storm its allotted space in time,
Quietly pursuing catastrophic histories buried in my eyes.
And yes, the world is not some unplayed Cosmic Game,
And the sun is still ninety-three million miles from me,
And in the imaginary forest, the shingled hippo becomes
        the gay unicorn.
No, my traffic is not with addled keepers of yesterday's
        disasters,
Seekers of manifest disembowelment on shafts of yesterday's
        pains.
Blues come dressed like introspective echoes of a journey.
And yes, I have searched the rooms of the moon on cold
        summer nights.
And yes, I have refought those unfinished encounters.
        Still, they remain unfinished.
And yes, I have at times wished myself something different.

The tragedies are sung nightly at the funerals of the poet;
The revisited soul is wrapped in the aura of familiarity.

African Dream / BOB KAUFMAN

In black core of night, it explodes
Silver thunder, rolling back my brain,
Bursting copper screens, memory worlds
Deep in star-fed beds of time,
Seducing my soul to diamond fires of night.
Faint outline, a ship—momentary fright
Lifted on waves of color,
Sunk in pits of light,
Drummed back through time,
Hummed back through mind,
Drumming, cracking the night.
Strange forest songs, skin sounds
Crashing through—no longer strange.
Incestuous yellow flowers tearing
Magic from the earth.
Moon-dipped rituals, led
By a scarlet god,
Caressed by ebony maidens
With daylight eyes,
Purple garments,
Noses that twitch,
Singing young girl songs
Of an ancient love
In dark, sunless places
Where memories are sealed,
Burned in eyes of tigers.

Suddenly wise, I fight the dream:
Green screams enfold my night.

Battle Report / BOB KAUFMAN

One thousand saxophones infiltrate the city,
Each with a man inside,
Hidden in ordinary cases,
Labeled FRAGILE.

A fleet of trumpets drops their hooks,
Inside at the outside.

Ten waves of trombones approach the city
Under blue cover
Of late autumn's neoclassical clouds.

Five hundred bassmen, all string feet tall,
Beating it back to the bass.

One hundred drummers, each a stick in each hand,
The delicate rumble of pianos, moving in.

The secret agent, an innocent bystander,
Drops a note in the wail box.

Five generals, gathered in the gallery,
Blowing plans.

At last, the secret code is flashed:
Now is the time, now is the time.

Attack: The sound of jazz.

The city falls.

Forget to Not / BOB KAUFMAN

Remember, poet, while gallivanting across the sky,
Skylarking, shouting, calling names . . . Walk softly.

Your footprint on rain clouds is visible to naked eyes,
Lamps barnacled to your feet refract the mirrored air.

Exotic scents of your hidden vision fly in the face of time.

Remember not to forget the dying colors of yesterday
As you inhale tomorrow's hot dream, blown from frozen lips.

Remember, you naked agent of every nothing.

Hearing James Brown at the Café des Nattes (Sidi-bou-Saïd, Tunisia) / RICHARD A. LONG

Yes, brother your word had come
                          Don't want nobody
                          Give me nuthin
Crowning this hilltop, long ago's lighthouse
                          Open up the do'
                          Git it myself
Your word comes, thanks to God and Marconi
To this eyrie where I sit
Mint tea before, serenaded by caged birds
And the undulating arias of Arabia,
Her last vestige of empire.

In waves, over the waves it comes
                          Don't want nobody
Mingling with birdsong and arabesques
                          Give me nuthin

Floating over an Andalusian mise en scène
(I remember Cordova)

                         Open up the do'
It pierces the blanched housetops, the waiting sea
                         Git it myself

You moan, Dido plunges into the flames
You groan, Hannibal embarks
You shriek, Cato's vow is fulfilled
You sigh, the sea roars beside a silent shore

Flaring into this moment
Your voice, snatched from beyond Sahara's sands
Crosses the western sea, enters familiarly
This concatenation of Africa's time
Flavoring mint, infusing birdsong, merging into the endless
vocalize.

Juan de Pareja: Painted by Velázquez

/ RICHARD A. LONG

(IN MEMORY OF ALAIN LOCKE)

Amused contempt, is it, that scintillates
       From your velvet domain
Or contempt for the bemused who throng
       The dim ascetic space?

Under the scrutiny of brown eyes and blue
       You view Rome's seven hills
Thinking, perhaps, of vacant yellow sands
       undulant, limitless.

Though chaotic and obscure the furies
       Who decree your present part,

Though anguished and confused the hungry eyes
     Feeding upon your flesh,
You mediate the sordid encounter,
     Osculant, putrid, rank
And regard, serene, the ceaseless discourse
     Of wisdom and folly.

If You Come Softly / AUDRE LORDE

If you come as softly
As wind within the trees
You may hear what I hear
See what sorrow sees.

If you come as lightly
As threading dew
I will take you gladly
Nor ask more of you.

You may sit beside me
Silent as a breath
Only those who stay dead
Shall remember death.

And if you come I will be silent
Nor speak harsh words to you.
I will not ask you why now.
Or how, or what you do.

We shall sit here, softly
Beneath two different years
And the rich earth between us
Shall drink our tears.

Young Negro Poet / CALVIN C. HERNTON

Young Negro poet
came from 'way down South,
Tennessee, to be exact,
   thought he had some verse,
   thought he could write,
   real well
   as a matter of fact.

Young Negro poet
came from 'way down South
up North,
New York City,
   found that he had no verse,
   couldn't write so well,
   folks back home had lied—
   what a pity, what a pity.

Young Negro poet
came from 'way down South
just to sleep on the cold ground,
Central Park,
to be exact . . .

     Wake up o jack-legged poet!
     Wake up o dark boy from 'way down South!
     Wake up out of Central Park, and walk
        through Harlem street.

     Walk down Seventh Avenue, Eighth,
     Madison, Lenox, and St. Nicholas,
     walk all around—
        it's morning in Harlem.

     Wake up jack-legged poet!
     Wake up dark boy from 'way down South!
     Wake up out of Central Park—
     wash your face in the fountain water,

take a long stretch,
    light up a cigarette butt, and walk defiantly
        through the streets of Harlem town.

Affirmation / HELEN ARMSTEAD JOHNSON

Barren cross-ties of penny-whistle twigs
Mating and parting as the wind
Beats the rhythm of sad songs
With black shafts once hung in gold.
Basketweave tears of ancestral black
Fall in arcs as the ruthless sun
Seeks the heart warm with traces
Which now the snow paints in crushing white.
But upward thrusts defy the requiem
And glisten in black affirmation
Of orchestrated songs to be sung tomorrow.

Philodendron / HELEN ARMSTEAD JOHNSON

I watch the calligraphy of shadows
Transform the evening wall
As the soft wind from the windows
Wafts secret patterns
To the split green leaves
Whose veins are only candle bright.

The ribless shapes
Join and cross,
Draining from memory
Other veinless, once green forms
That joined and crossed
Before eroding days
Etched split green patterns,
Which even now
Inform the evening wall
In candlelight.

Woman with Flower / NAOMI LONG MADGETT

I wouldn't coax the plant if I were you.
Such watchful nurturing may do it harm.
Let the soil rest from so much digging
And wait until it's dry before you water it.
The leaf's inclined to find its own direction;
Give it a chance to seek the sunlight for itself.

Much growth is stunted by too careful prodding,
Too eager tenderness.
The things we love we have to learn to leave alone.

Good Times / LUCILLE CLIFTON

My Daddy has paid the rent
and the insurance man is gone
and the lights is back on
and my uncle Brud has hit
for one dollar straight
and they is good times
good times
good times

My Mama has made bread
and Grampaw has come
and everybody is drunk
and dancing in the kitchen
and singing in the kitchen
oh these is good times
good times
good times

oh children think about the
good times

Malcolm X—An Autobiography / LARRY NEAL

I am the Seventh Son of the Son
who was also the Seventh.
I have drunk deep of the waters of my ancestors
have travelled the soul's journey towards cosmic harmony
the Seventh Son.
Have walked slick avenues
and seen grown men, fall, to die in a blue doom

of death and ancestral agony,
have seen old men glide, shadowless, feet barely
touching the pavements.

I sprung out of the Midwestern plains
the bleak Michigan landscape, the black blues of Kansas
City, the kiss-me-nights.
out of the bleak Michigan landscape wearing the slave name—
Malcolm Little.
Saw a brief vision in Lansing, when I was seven, and in
my mother's womb heard the beast cry of death,
a landscape on which white robed figures ride, and my
Garvey father silhouetted against the night-fire, gun in hand,
form outlined against a panorama of violence.

Out of the Midwestern bleakness, I sprang, pushed eastward,
past shack on country nigger shack, across the wilderness
of North America.

I hustler. I pimp. I unfulfilled black man
bursting with destiny.
New York City Slim called me Big Red,
and there was no escape, close nights of the smell of death.
Pimp. hustler. The day fills these rooms.
I am talking about New York. Harlem.
talking about the neon madness.
talking about ghetto eyes and nights
about death protruding across the room. Small's paradise.
talking about cigarette butts, and rooms smelly with white
sex flesh, and dank sheets, and being on the run.

talking about cocaine illusions, about stealing and selling.
talking about these New York cops who smell of blood and
          money.
I am Big Red, tiger vicious, Big Red, bad nigger, will kill.

But there is rhythm here. Its own special substance:
I hear Billie sing, no good man, and dig Prez, wearing the
          Zoot

suit of life—the porkpie hat tilted at the correct angle.
through the Harlem smoke of beer and whiskey, I understand
    the
mystery of the signifying monkey,
in a blue haze of inspiration, I reach to the totality of Being.
I am at the center of a swirl of events. War and death.
rhythm. hot women. I think life a commodity bargained for
across the bar in Small's.
I perceive the echoes of Bird and there is a gnawing in the
    maw
of my emotions.
and then there is jail. America is the world's greatest jailer,
and we all in jails. black spirits contained like magnificent
birds of wonder. I now understand my father urged on by the
ghost of Garvey,
and see a small brown man standing in a corner. The cell.
    cold.
dank. The light around him vibrates. Am I crazy? But to
    under-
stand is to submit to a more perfect will, a more perfect order.
To understand is to surrender the imperfect self
for a more perfect self.

Allah formed brown man, I follow
and shake within the very depth of my most imperfect being,
and I bear witness to the Message of Allah
and I bear witness—all praise is due Allah!

But He Was Cool
or: he even stopped for green lights
Don L. Lee

super-cool
ultrablack
a tan/purple
had a beautiful shade.

he had a double-natural
that wd put the sisters to shame.
his dashikis were tailor made
& his beads were imported sea shells
    (from some blk/country i never heard of)
he was triple-hip.

his tikis were hand carved
out of ivory
& came express from the motherland.
he would greet u in swahili
& say good-by in yoruba.
woooooooooooo-jim he bes so cool & ill tel li gent
        cool-cool is so cool he was un-cooled by
                other niggers' cool
        cool-cool ultracool was bop-cool/ice box
                cool so cool cold cool
        his wine didn't have to be cooled, him was
                air conditioned cool
        cool-cool/real cool made me cool—now
                ain't that cool
        cool-cool so cool him nick-named refrigerator.

cool-cool so cool
he didn't know,

after detroit, newark, chicago &c.,
we had to hip
        cool-cool/ super-cool/ real cool
   that

to be black
is
to be
very-hot.

Assassination / Don L. Lee

it was wild.
the
bullet hit high.
          (the throat-neck)
& from everywhere:
    the motel, from under bushes and cars,
    from around corners and across streets,
    out of the garbage cans and from rat holes
    in the earth
they came running
with
guns
drawn
they came running
toward the King—
          all of them
          fast and sure—
as if
the King
was going to fire back.
they came running,
fast and sure,
in the
wrong
direction.

Education / DON L. LEE

I had a good teacher,
He taught me everything I know;
how to lie,
      cheat,
          and how to strike the softest blow.

My teacher thought himself to be wise and right
He taught me things most people consider nice;
      such as to pray,
             smile,
              and how not to fight.

My teacher taught me other things too,
Things that I will be forever looking at;
      how to berate,
          segregate,
          and how to be inferior without hate.

My teacher's wisdom forever grows,
He taught me things every child will know;
      how to steal,
          appeal,
          and accept most things against my will.

All these acts take as facts,
The mistake was made in teaching me
How not to be BLACK.

Stereo / Don L. Lee

I can clear a beach or swimming pool without
       touching water.
I can make a lunch counter become deserted
       in less than an hour.
I can make property value drop by being seen
       in a realtor's tower.
I ALONE can make the word of God have little
       or no meaning to many
       in Sunday morning's prayer hour.
I have Power.
BLACK POWER.

My Poem / Nikki Giovanni

i am 25 years old
black female poet
wrote a poem asking
nigger can you kill
if they kill me
it won't stop
the revolution

i have been robbed
it looked like they knew
that i was to be hit
they took my tv
my two rings
my piece of african print
and my two guns

202

if they take my life
it won't stop
the revolution

my phone is tapped
my mail is opened
they've caused me to turn
on all my old friends
and all my new lovers
if i hate all black
people
and all negroes
it won't stop
the revolution

i'm afraid to tell
my roommate where i'm going
and scared to tell
people if i'm coming
if i sit here
for the rest
of my life
it won't stop
the revolution

if i never write
another poem
or short story
if i flunk out
of grad school
if my car is reclaimed
and my record player
won't play
and if i never see
a peaceful day
or do a meaningful
black thing
it won't stop
the revolution

the revolution
is in the streets
and if i stay on
the 5th floor
it will go on

Nikki-Rosa / Nikki Giovanni

childhood remembrances are always a drag
if you're Black
you always remember things like living in Woodlawn
with no inside toilet
and if you become famous or something
they never talk about how happy you were to have your
          mother
all to yourself and
how good the water felt when you got your bath from one of
          those
big tubs that folk in Chicago barbecue in
and somehow when you talk about home
it never gets across how much you
understood their feelings
as the whole family attended meetings about Hollydale
and even though you remember
your biographers never understand
your father's pain as he sells his stock
and another dream goes
and though you're poor it isn't poverty that
concerns you
and though they fought a lot
it isn't your father's drinking that makes any difference
but only that everybody is together and you

and your sister have happy birthdays and very good
    christmases
and I really hope no white person ever has cause to write
    about me
because they never understand Black love is Black wealth and
    they'll
probably talk about my hard childhood and never understand
    that
all the while I was quite happy

Knoxville, Tennessee / NIKKI GIOVANNI

I always like summer
best
you can eat fresh corn
from daddy's garden
and okra
and greens
and cabbage
and lots of
barbecue
and buttermilk
and homemade ice-cream
at the church picnic
and listen to
gospel music
outside
at the church
homecoming
and go to the mountains with
your grandmother
and go barefooted

and be warm
all the time
not only when you go to bed
and sleep

The Funeral of Martin Luther King, Jr.
NIKKI GIOVANNI

His headstone said
FREE AT LAST, FREE AT LAST
But death is a slave's freedom
We seek the freedom of free men
And the construction of a world
Where Martin Luther King could have lived and
    preached non-violence

Kidnap Poem / NIKKI GIOVANNI

ever been kidnapped
by a poet
if i were a poet
i'd kidnap you
put you in my phrases and meter
you to jones beach
or maybe coney island
or maybe just to my house

206

lyric you in lilacs
dash you in the rain
blend into the beach
to complement my sea
play the lyre for you
ode you with my love song
anything to win you
wrap you in the red Black green
show you off to mama
yeah if i were a poet i'd kid
nap you

A Robin's Poem / NIKKI GIOVANNI

if you plant grain
you get fields of flour
if you plant seeds
you get grass
or babies
i planted once
and a robin red breast flew
in my window
but a tom cat wouldn't let it
stay

No Smiles / FRANK LAMONT PHILLIPS

We are with one another
sometimes
and there are no smiles
no easy togetherness
only one and one
against the grain
we speak
sometimes and
nothing
is said
but where we are
apart
there is longing
and pain
like arguments within
ourselves
that will not end

Genealogy / FRANK LAMONT PHILLIPS

The magnolia trees
that blossom in summer sun
on summer days
in the south
have my mother's name
written
on each leaf
where her hands
touched saplings that tore

208

my back
long ago in summer heat
after day
when mama bent
over cotton plant
and sang
in fields where her
mama had worked
before she was born
and had sung
songs too
full of grief for tears

Maryuma / Frank Lamont Phillips

at seventeen your
thoughts were younger
than your face
and your smile
mirrored in dishwater
was mississippi pleasant
you had large eyes
and larger hopes of marrying
somebody rich
or famous or something
you settled for a little house
so close to the tracks
that the sound of a train shook
some of everything
you settled for a boy
with eyes larger than
your own

you settled for dishwater
just as deep
as that you knew
at home

And She Was Bad / MARVIN WYCHE, JR.

she slid past
so fly & outtasight
that whistles
didn't phase her
her strut putting   roosters
to shame
had a keyhole figure
that would open any door
had knobs
that would turn any head
she was   bad   jack
awww she was fly

she had the brown   est of eyes
matching a smooth ebony complexion
glimpsed now and then
through tons of cream-style
makeup
her dress was mini's mammy
revealed   beaucoup booty
and her stockings changed colors
every five miles.
she was decorated in
silver-dipped jew els
imported from
                    jap—an

her fingernails
were miniature
rainbows
man she was up on   all
the latest fashions
cause she was bad
yeah she was fly

her afro wig
was shaped
to bring out its fullll
      naturalness???
her lips were painted by
max factor   himself

myself
scoped her   and said:

      hey sister
      like whuss your name?

and she looked around
to see if my   SISTER

was as bad
as she was

We Rainclouds / MARVIN WYCHE, JR.

black people, we rainclouds

closer to the sun and full of life.
soaking up the knowledge of the earth
                              and

storing it within ourselves
                              moving on
to spread truth throughout the world

we black clouds.
loved and feared.
ready to explode and give new life
to a dying planet

beautiful dark clouds
casting shadows of blackness
shadows of dignity
shadows of
                    love

giving of ourselves to promote life
                                        while

realizing our ability to destroy

rainclouds
              we are
nature
nature
nature

natural!!!
black people, we rainclouds

closer to the sun and full of life

Leslie / MARVIN WYCHE, JR.

that same look.
eyes wide in puzzlement
confusion.

you wonder why
i act the way
i do
and i wonder
why
you think i'm acting

Five Sense / Marvin Wyche, Jr.

morning.
and she awoke to
see
the same sameness:

       basement bedroom
       dusty mirror
       scattered cosmetics

       half empty double bed

she awoke   to
smell
the plastic flowers
on the dresser
(a gift of an ancient anniversary)
and her memories
became
tears   defiantly tracing
her
swelling
brown
cheeks

she awoke
to   hear
herself cussing
cussing
a nickel hearted absence
sour/sweet thought
that
nickel hearted
absence
she awoke
to   taste
the bitter loneliness
of life
without her man

morning.
and she awoke
to   feel

forgotten

Biographical Notes

Index of Titles

Acknowledgments

Biographical Notes

The following biographical notes were written by Arna Bontemps. The publishers have taken the liberty of adding new information about the careers of the contributors after Bontemps's death in 1973. Special thanks go to Raquel Coghill of the Schomburg Center for Research in Black Culture at the New York Public Library for her work on this edition.

SAMUEL ALLEN (1917–   ) was one of James Weldon Johnson's students of creative writing at Fisk University. He also attended Harvard Law School and has studied at the Sorbonne in Paris, where Richard Wright discovered his poetry and had it published in *Présence Africaine*. A collection of his poems, *Elfenbein Zänne (Ivory Tusks)*, signed Paul Vesey, was brought out in 1956 by Wolfgang Rothe Verlag in Heidelberg. Allen has been connected with the Legal Department of the United States Information Agency and has taught at Tuskegee Institute, Wesleyan University, and Boston University, and has compiled an anthology of African poetry. His other publications include *Poems* and *Voice Not Our Own*. He is Professor Emeritus of African American history at Boston University.

RUSSELL ATKINS (1926–   ) has had poems in avant-garde journals since the 1940s. He still lives in Cleveland, Ohio, the city where he was born and educated. *Free Lance*, which he founded in 1950 and ran until 1979, is considered the most significant avant-garde publication of poetry and prose of the period and is probably the oldest black-owned literary magazine in the United States. Atkins's later books of poetry are *Here in The* (1976) and *Whichever* (1978).

GWENDOLYN B. BENNETT (1902–81), born in Giddings, Texas, attended elementary school in Washington, D.C., before moving on to Girls' High School in Brooklyn, New York, where she was graduated in 1921. Subsequently, she studied at Columbia University and at Brooklyn's Pratt Institute. An early interest in the fine arts also led to study at the Académie Julian and the École de Panthéon in Paris. From 1926 to 1928 she wrote a regularly featured column, "The Ebony Flute," for *Opportunity*, chronicling the activities of the cultural leaders of the Harlem Renaissance. She taught art at Howard University, and was selected as one of two African American artists to study the Barnes Foundation's collection of modern and primitive art.

HORACE JULIAN BOND (1940–   ) has lived for most of his life in Atlanta, Georgia, as did his late father, Dr. Horace Mann Bond. He took an active part in the student movement that was responsible for sit-ins and other attacks on segregation in his home city, which casts a sidelight on his often-quoted couplet:

> Look at that gal shake that thing—
> We can't all be Martin Luther King.

Since that campaign, he won a seat in the Georgia Legislature, had it denied him, had the denial overruled; and had his name placed in nomination for Vice-President of the United States, even though he was too young to qualify. His book *A Time to Speak, A Time to Act* was published in 1972. Bond has taught history and politics at the American University, University of Virginia, and Harvard and Drexel universities. Between 1965 and 1987 he served in both the House of Representatives and the Senate, representing Georgia. Today he hosts *American Black Forum*, a syndicated television news program based in Washington, D.C.

217

WILLIAM STANLEY BRAITHWAITE (1878–1962) was born in Boston, of West Indian parents. His career as a poet began in 1904 with the publication of *Lyrics of Life and Love*. A second volume, *The House of Falling Leaves*, followed two years later. In 1946, his *Selected Poems* appeared. Between 1913 and 1929 Braithwaite edited an annual *Anthology of Magazine Verse* and presented the work of American poets such as Edgar Lee Masters, Vachel Lindsay, and Carl Sandburg before they were widely recognized. He also edited other general anthologies and served on the editorial staff of the *Boston Transcript*.

GWENDOLYN BROOKS (1917–   ), awarded the Pulitzer Prize for poetry in 1959 for *Annie Allen*, has since written fiction as well as verse for children and more poetry. Her first collection, *A Street in Bronzeville*, was published in 1945; *The Bean Eaters* in 1961. She read her poems for the National Poetry Festival at the Library of Congress in 1962. She won the Friends Literary Award for Poetry in 1964 and taught poetry at Northeastern Illinois State College; Columbia College, Chicago; and Elmhurst College, Elmhurst, Illinois. She was named Poet Laureate of Illinois, succeeding Carl Sandburg. Her other works include *Jump Bad: A New Chicago Anthology* and *The World of Gwendolyn Brooks*, both published in 1971. More recent works include *The Near-Johannesburg Boy, and Other Poems* (1986) and *Children Coming Home* (1991). She now holds more than fifty honorary degrees and from 1985 to 1986 served as Consultant in Poetry to the Library of Congress.

JONATHAN BROOKS (1904–45) and his widowed mother worked a sharecroppers' farm in Mississippi until he was fourteen, when he began the uphill struggle for an education. When he died in 1945, he was working in the post office at Corinth. *The Resurrection and Other Poems*, his only book, was published posthumously.

STERLING A. BROWN (1901–89) had a distinguished career as a member of the faculty of Howard University. Educated in the schools of Washington, D.C., and at Williams College and Harvard University, he taught at Fisk University and Lincoln University in Missouri before beginning the long association with Howard which led to his selection in 1961 to write a history of that university. His published books include *Southern Road* (1932), a volume of poetry; *The Negro in American Fiction* (1938); and *Negro Poetry and Drama* (1938). He served as senior editor of *Negro Caravan*, first published in 1941 and revised in 1969. In 1984 he was named Poet Laureate of the District of Columbia. *The Collected Poems of Sterling Brown* was published in 1980.

WILLIAM BROWNE (1923–   ) was born in New York. A student of clinical psychology, he traveled widely, worked at many jobs, and occasionally published poems in the *Pittsburgh Courier*. His poems have also been published in the anthology *Beyond the Blues* and the journal *Présence Africaine*.

CATHERINE CATER (1917–   ), daughter of a college dean, holds academic degrees from Talladega College in Alabama and the University of Michigan. She has been a librarian and a professor of English.

MARCUS B. CHRISTIAN (1900–76), a self-educated printer-poet and Louisiana history buff, wrote for the Negro History Unit of the Federal Writers' Project in New Orleans. His poems and articles appeared in anthologies and periodicals, and a book, *High Ground*, was printed on his own press in New Orleans in 1958, commemorating the U.S. Supreme Court's decision of May 17, 1954. His last book was *Negro Ironworkers of Louisiana*, published in 1972. He taught African American history at Dillard and Louisiana State universities, and was also a frequent contributor to *Opportunity* and *Louisiana Weekly*.

LUCILLE CLIFTON (1936–   ) was born in Depew, New York, and attended Howard University and Fredonia State Teachers College. She is married and the mother of six children. Her collection of poems, *Good Times* (1969), included some poems previously published in *The Massachusetts Review*. She has also written *Some of the*

218

Days of Everett Anderson (1970), *Good News About the Earth* (1972), and *Everett Anderson's Christmas Coming* (1972). *Ordinary Woman* (1974) and *Quilting Poems 1987–1990* (1991) secured Clifton's reputation as a highly gifted writer. She was named Poet Laureate of Maryland, nominated for a Pulitzer Prize for poetry, and awarded two grants from the NEA.

LESLIE M. COLLINS (1914–   ), born in Alexandria, Louisiana, was educated by the Sisters of St. James before he attended Straight College and Dillard University in New Orleans. He holds advanced degrees from Fisk and Western Reserve universities and taught for eight years before joining the English faculty at Fisk in 1945.

COUNTEE CULLEN's (1903–46) literary talents developed in the parsonage of a large church in Harlem. Reared by foster parents, he won poetry prizes as well as scholastic honors at Dewitt Clinton High School and at New York University. Before graduating in 1925, he had already had poems published in leading magazines and his first book, *Color*, had appeared. A graduate degree from Harvard followed. Then in 1927 two more collections of poetry were published, *Copper Sun* and *The Ballad of the Brown Girl*. *The Black Christ* (1929) was written in France on a Guggenheim Fellowship. His other books include *One Way to Heaven* (1932), a novel; *The Medea and Other Poems* (1935); *The Lost Zoo* (1940); *My Nine Lives and How I Lost Them* (1942); and *On These I Stand*, which appeared posthumously in 1947. Cullen edited *Caroling Dusk* (1927), an anthology of American Negro poetry, and collaborated with Arna Bontemps in the dramatization of *St. Louis Woman*, from Bontemps's novel *God Sends Sunday* (1931). The latest publication of his work is *My Soul's High Song: The Collected Writings of Countee Cullen, Voice of the Harlem Renaissance* (1991).

WARING CUNEY (1906–76) attended schools and conservatories in Washington, D.C., his birthplace, and Pennsylvania, Boston, and Rome. While he was still a student at Lincoln University, his "No Images" won a national poetry contest. It was widely reprinted in 1926 and has often been anthologized, as have some of his later poems. Several of his poems of protest, sung by Josh White, were recorded and issued as an album under the title *Southern Exposure*. Cuney's later success was in Europe; in 1960 his *Puzzles* was published in Holland, and in 1976 *Store Front Church* appeared in London.

MARGARET DANNER (1915–   ) was born in Pryorsburg, Kentucky, but has spent the greater part of her life in Chicago, where she was at one time associated with *Poetry: The Magazine of Verse*. A selection of her poems appearing in that magazine prompted the John Hay Whitney Opportunity Fellowships Committee to offer her a trip to Africa. In 1962 the literary group with which she was associated in Detroit was featured in a special issue of the *Bulletin of Negro History*. She is interested in French and African art, and published a collection of verse in 1968 entitled *Iron Lace*. In that same year she received an award from Poets in Concert, and in 1970 she was poet-in-residence at Virginia Union University in Richmond. Her second volume of poetry was *The Down of a Thistle: Selected Poems, Prose Poems, and Songs*.

FRANK MARSHALL DAVIS (1905–87) left a career in journalism, mainly with the Associated Negro Press, for the tropical attractions of Hawaii, where he lived with his family. Four volumes of his free verse (Chicago style) were published: *Black Man's Verse* (1935), *I Am the American Negro* (1937), *47th Street* (1948), and *Awakening and Other Poems* (1978).

CLARISSA SCOTT DELANY (1901–27), beautiful and talented, was a magazine cover girl the year she was graduated from Wellesley. She was a teacher in Dunbar High School in Washington, D.C., when she married Hubert Delany in 1926. Her literary reviews and poetry appeared in *Opportunity*.

OWEN DODSON (1914–83) was head of the Department of Drama at Howard University in Washington, D.C. A graduate of Bates College and Yale University, he had two of his plays, *Divine Comedy* and *Garden of Time*, produced at Yale while he was working toward his Fine Arts degree. Others were presented on other campuses, and in 1946 a collection of his poems, *Powerful Long Ladder*, was published. In 1967 he received a Doctor of Letters from Bates, and during the spring of 1969 he was poet-in-residence at the University of Arizona. His books of poetry include *Cages* (1953), *Confession Stone* (1970), and *The Harlem Book of the Dead* (with James Van Der Zee and Camille Bishops) (1978).

ALFRED A. DUCKETT (1918–84) was a public-relations man in New York and had broad experience in journalism, with the *Amsterdam News*, *New York Age*, and *Pittsburgh Courier*. His early poems occasionally reappear in anthologies, and he was the author of *Changing of the Guard: The New Black Breed of Black Politicians*, published in 1972.

PAUL LAURENCE DUNBAR (1872–1906) was discovered operating an elevator in Dayton, Ohio, in 1893. One might almost say a new era began that year for the American Negro in literary expression. His *Oak and Ivy*, privately printed in 1893, attracted little attention, and his *Majors and Minors* (1895) made a similarly small impression, but together they paved the way for *Lyrics of a Lowly Life* (1896). This book won for the poet a national reputation and enabled him to pursue a literary career for the rest of his life. A Negro poet had not won recognition in the United States in the century and a quarter since the family of John Wheatly of Boston emancipated their slave girl, Phillis, in recognition of her *Poems on Various Subjects, Religious and Moral* (1773). Dunbar's life was short, as was Phillis's: both suffered from tuberculosis. In spite of illness, Dunbar wrote prose as well as poetry in the decade following *Lyrics*, and his *Complete Poems* (1913) has retained a warm appeal for many readers.

JAMES A. EMANUEL's (1921–   ) doctoral dissertation at Columbia University in 1962 was concerned with the short stories of Langston Hughes. Emanuel's poems have appeared in *Phylon* and other magazines and newspapers. He taught at the City College of the City University of New York. His works include *Dark Symphony: Negro Literature in America* (1968), *Treehouse and Other Poems* (1968), *Panther Man* (1970), *A Chisel in the Dark* (1980), and *The Broken Bowl* (1983).

MARI E. EVANS (1923–   ), born and raised in Toledo, Ohio, was a John Hay Whitney Fellow in 1965–66. Her poetry has appeared extensively in textbooks and anthologies. Producer/director of a weekly half-hour television series, she has also been writer-in-residence and instructor in Black Literature at Indiana University and Purdue University. In 1970 she published *I Am a Black Woman*. Evans's recent poetic works, such as *Nightstar: 1973–1978* (1982) and *A Dark and Splendid Mass* (1992), her books for adolescents, her work for television and other media, and her volume on black female writers 1950–1980, have ensured her a lasting place among the champions of African American literature. Between 1989 and 1990 she was Writer in Residence at Spelman College.

JULIA FIELDS (1938–   ) returned to her native Alabama to teach high school in the steel city of Bessemer after she graduated from Knoxville College in Tennessee. But her first summer vacation after her return was spent in a very different setting—the Bread Loaf Writers' Conference in New England. She published a collection, *Poems*, in 1968, and her work has also appeared in *Massachusetts Review*, *Riverside Poetry II*, *Beyond the Blues*, *New Negro Poets*, and *Negro Digest*. Fields has taught at Howard University and Hampton Institute, and in 1979 founded the Learning School of American Language. Other collections include *East of Moonlight* (1973), *A Summoning, A Shining* (1976), and *Slow Coins* (1981).

NIKKI GIOVANNI (1943–   ) was born in Knoxville, Tennessee, and educated at Fisk University in Nashville. She has been associated with Rutgers University, has contributed poems to various black publications, has read poems on educational television and published several collections of poetry, including *Black Judgement* (1968). She is also the author of *Gemini* (1972), a volume of prose. Giovanni's poetry, which has a multigenerational and international readership, is concerned with family, blackness, womanhood, and sex, and is influenced strongly by rhythm and blues music. Since the 1970s she has published many poetry collections, notably *My House* and *Cotton Candy on a Rainy Day.*

YVONNE GREGORY (1919–   ) frequently contributed poems to the *Fisk Herald* when she was an undergraduate. Since then, her occasional appearances in magazines have all been in prose.

ANGELINA W. GRIMKÉ (1880–1958) spent the last years of her life in quiet retirement in New York City, but before that she had been for many years a teacher of English in the Washington, D.C., high schools. Her three-act play, *Rachel*, was published in 1921.

ROBERT HAYDEN (1913–80), born in Detroit, attended Wayne State University and the University of Michigan, where for two years he held a teaching assistantship. In 1938 and again in 1942, he received Avery Hopwood Awards for poetry at Michigan; and in 1940 a collection of his poems, *Heartshape in the Dust*, was published in Detroit. In 1946 he joined the faculty of Fisk University, where his teaching was occasionally interrupted by fellowships for creative writing. His poems appeared in *Poetry, The Atlantic Monthly*, and other periodicals and anthologies. A brochure, *The Lion and the Archer* (1948), presented a group of his poems with some of Myron O'Higgins's. *A Ballad of Remembrance* (1962) was published in London and won first prize at the First World Festival of Negro Arts, held in 1965 in Dakar, Senegal. In the United States, he published *Selected Poems* (1966), *Kaleidoscope* (1967), and *Words in the Mourning Time* (1970). He was visiting professor of English at the University of Michigan in 1968, and at the University of Louisville, Kentucky, in 1969. Hayden's knowledge of African American life and culture and of forms outside that culture enabled him to write strikingly rich and memorable poems. Today he is considered one of the most talented American poets of the century. In 1970 he won the Russell Liones Award, and in 1975 was elected to the American Academy of Poets. In 1976 he was the first black man appointed as Consultant in Poetry to the Library of Congress. His later works include *The Night Blooming Cereus* (1972), *Angle of Ascent: New and Selected Poems* (1975), and *American Journal* (1978).

DONALD JEFFREY HAYES's (1904–91) greatest interest was in music as well as poetry, but beyond high school his education was gained through private study. He worked for many years as a counselor with the New Jersey State Employment Service in Atlantic City. His poems appeared in *Harper's Bazaar, Good Housekeeping*, and *This Week*, and some were set to music.

CALVIN C. HERNTON (1932–   ) is a native of Chattanooga, Tennessee. He studied sociology at Talledega College in Alabama (B.A., 1954) and at Fisk University (M.A., 1956). He has taught at other, previously all-black colleges in the South and has been employed by the New York Welfare Department. His poems were first published in *Phylon* (1954), but he has been writing since his early teens. His prose writings include *Sex and Racism in America* (1965). A book of his poetry appeared in a limited edition in 1964 under the title *The Coming of Chonos to the House of Nightsong: An Epical Narrative of the South.* He has written many books, including *Coming Together: Black Power, White Hatred, and Sexual Hangups* (1971); *Scarecrow*, a novel (1974); *Medicine Man*, poems (1976); and *Sexual Mountains and Black Women Writers: Adventures in Sex, Literature, and Real Life* (1987). He is Professor of Black Studies at Oberlin College.

CARL WENDELL HINES, JR. (1940–79), had his own jazz combo and played for dances as a student at Tennessee Agricultural and Industrial University, where Wilma Rudolph, Ralph Boston, and other Olympic athletes studied. Not until he graduated in 1962, however, was his real secret revealed: he had been writing some of the most authentic jazz poetry of this period. He was a native of Wilson, North Carolina, and went to A. & I. to study engineering but switched to science education. He never studied music formally.

M. CARL HOLMAN (1919–) was president of the National Urban Coalition in Washington, D.C., in the late 1960s. A native of Minter City, Mississippi, Holman spent his youth in St. Louis. He holds academic degrees from Lincoln University in Missouri, the University of Chicago, and Yale University. While at Chicago, he won a Fiske Poetry Prize and was granted a Rosenwald Fellowship for advanced study in creative writing. Since 1949, Holman has taught at Clark College in Atlanta, Atlanta University, and Hampton Institute in Virginia. From 1960 to 1963 he was editor of the *Atlanta Inquirer*. Before joining the Coalition he was a member of the U.S. Commission on Civil Rights.

FRANK HORNE (1899–1974) was a New Yorker. The background of his widely reprinted poem "To James" would seem to be his own experience on the track team of the College of the City of New York. His subsequent career included graduate and professional studies at the Northern Illinois College of Ophthalmology, Columbia University, and the University of Southern California. As a Doctor of Optometry, he practiced in Chicago and New York. A period of college teaching followed before he began the long and distinguished service in government which earned him prestige as a leading authority on housing. He contributed to *Opportunity*, *The Crisis*, and *Carolina* magazines. *Haverstraw*, a collection of his poetry, was published in 1963.

LANGSTON HUGHES (1902–67) wrote poetry, plays, and short stories, as well as *The Big Sea* and *I Wonder As I Wander: An Autobiographical Journey*. He began writing poetry as a student at Central High in Cleveland, Ohio, and even before he graduated from Lincoln University in Pennsylvania, he was supporting himself by writing. His public readings of his poetry, which began after the publication of *The Weary Blues*, his first book, in 1926, were always warmly received. Langston Hughes also wrote novels, newspaper columns, books for children, song lyrics, and even works of historical interest, including the story of the NAACP. He held Guggenheim and Rosenwald fellowships and an American Academy of Arts and Letters grant. The Free Academy of Arts in Hamburg honored him in 1964, and Emperior Haile Selassie of Ethiopia decorated him in 1966. Two of the last books published before his death are *Simple's Uncle Sam* (1965) and *The Sweet Flypaper of Life* (1967).

TED JOANS (1928–) was born Theodore Jones on a riverboat at Cairo, Illinois, on July 4, just after the annual street parade ended. Twelve years later to the hour, he recalls, his riverboat-entertainer father put a trumpet in his hands and ushered him off the boat at Memphis. A wanderer thereafter, Ted somehow managed to stay put long enough to get a degree from Indiana University. In 1951, he says, he "joined the Bohemia of Greenwich Village, U.S.A." His painting and poetry have been exhibited and published, often in connection with the Beat Generation. His works include *Black Pow-Wow* (1969) and *Afrodisia: New Poems by Ted Joans* (1971). Along with Amiri Baraka, Bob Kaufman, Jack Kerouac, and Allen Ginsberg, Joans is recognized today as one of the creators of the Beat Generation. In 1961 he bid farewell to overcommercialized America to travel through Africa and Europe. As an ex-patriot, he gave American readers of poetry a unique perspective on their culture with works such as *A Black Manifesto in Jazz Poetry and Prose* (1971).

FENTON JOHNSON (1888–1958) was once a dapper fellow who drove his own electric automobile around Chicago at the end of the first decade of this century. Since he was an only child in a family of some means, he was able to pursue his interest in the arts. One of these was writing and producing plays at the old Pekin Theatre on South

State Street. Another was editing and publishing little magazines. More enduring than either of these, however, was his love for poetry. His first collection, *A Little Dreaming*, came out in 1914. *Visions of the Dusk* and other volumes strongly influenced by Paul Laurence Dunbar followed in the next few years. By the 1920s, times had changed for the Johnsons, and young Fenton succumbed to a more rugged influence, which showed in his later verse, including the posthumously published *42 WPA Poems*. His third and last volume of poetry was *Songs of Soil* (1916).

GEORGIA DOUGLAS JOHNSON (1877–1966) was born in Atlanta, Georgia. She studied music at Oberlin Conservatory in Ohio but soon gave up her early ambition to become a composer. She had been working as a schoolteacher when her husband was appointed Recorder of Deeds under President William Howard Taft and they moved to Washington, D.C. Later she was employed in government agencies, but writing became her principal occupation. Published collections of her lyrics include *The Heart of a Woman* (1918), *Bronze* (1922), *An Autumn Love Cycle* (1928), and *Share My World* (1962). Overlooked for years, Johnson is now considered an important figure in the development of African American literature and in the New Negro Renaissance. The literary salon she held in her Washington home—the Round Table—was attended by scores of black intellectuals, including W.E.B. Du Bois, Angelina Weld Grimké, and Zora Neale Hurston.

HELEN ARMSTEAD JOHNSON (1920–) was a professor of English at York College of the City University of New York. She earned a Ph.D. degree and was considered a specialist in black-theater history, particularly for her article "Black Theater: 1960 and After" in *The Afro-American Reference Book* (1973). She was also a Fellow of the School of Letters at Indiana University.

HELENE JOHNSON (1907–95), born in Boston, was the youngest of the young poets and writers who brought about the Negro Renaissance, as it was called in Harlem in the 1920s. She contributed to *Opportunity: A Journal of Negro Life*, *Vanity Fair*, and other magazines.

JAMES WELDON JOHNSON (1871–1938) created "small literary works, unpretentious but remarkably durable, in a variety of forms." His autobiography, *Along This Way* (1933), however, is a large and enlightening work. He often observed that the years of his life seemed to move in cycles of seven, and these included periods of high-school teaching and administration, diplomatic service as a U.S. Consul in Latin America, an exciting seven years as a lyricist on Broadway, a notable span as Executive Secretary of the National Association for the Advancement of Colored People, and a final phase as professor of Creative Literature at Fisk University. But poetry was the thread that pulled all of them together. Johnson was born in Jacksonville, Florida. His books of poetry include *Fifty Years and Other Poems* (1917), *God's Trombones* (1927), and *St. Peter Relates an Incident* (1930). His best-known work of fiction is *The Autobiography of an Ex-Coloured Man*, which was first published in 1912.

LEROI JONES (Amiri Baraka) (1934–) has contributed to a number of publications, including *Yugen*, his own avant-garde magazine. His first collection was a paperback called *Preface to a Twenty Volume Suicide Note* (1961); his second was *The Dead Lecturer* (1963). Among other recognitions of promise, he received a John Hay Whitney Opportunity Fellowship for creative writing. He also received a Guggenheim Fellowship in 1964–65, and his plays and productions have won several awards, including an Obie for *Dutchman* in 1964 and an International Art Festival Prize at Dakar, Senegal, in 1966. His publications include *Home* (1966), *Black Magic and Tales* (1967), *Raise Race Rays Raze* (1972), and *African Congress: A Documentary of the First Modern Pan-African Congress* (1972). He has taught at the New School for Social Research and at Columbia University, and he founded the Black Arts Repertory Theatre School in Harlem and the Spirit House Movers and Players in Newark.

223

Recently he has published *Reggae or Not! Poems* (1982) and *The Autobiography of LeRoi Jones* (1984). He is a professor in the Department of African Studies at the State University of New York at Stony Brook.

BOB KAUFMAN (1925–) was published in *Broadsides* by City Lights in San Francisco as early as 1959 and 1960. The first collection of his poems was *Golden Sardine* (1967), published by the same company. In 1965, his poetry of the previous ten years and some of his prose were collected in *Solitudes Crowded with Loneliness*. Kaufman himself, a member of the San Francisco group of poets who made the "renaissance of the 1950s" in that city, dropped out of sight just as his poetry began to win a wider audience. In France he has been called the "Black American Rimbaud," and his reputation is even greater in Europe than in the United States. His *Watch My Tracks* was published in 1971, followed by *Ancient Rain: Poems 1956–1978* (1981).

DON L. LEE (Haki R. Madhubuti) (1942–) was born in Little Rock, Arkansas, but was reared and educated in Chicago. His *Think Black!* (1967) was a sensation of the "new Black consciousness," and it was followed by quick reprints and revisions as well as other collections of poetry: *Black Pride* (1968), *Don't Cry, Scream* (1969), and *We Walk the Way of the New World* (1970). Lee has been a writer-in-residence at Cornell University and a teacher at several other universities and colleges, especially in the Chicago area. As editor of Third World Press, he puts out a bibliographical magazine, *Black Books Bulletin*, and publishes broadsides and books. He also edited, with James A. Emanuel, *Dynamite Voices: Black Poets of the 1960's* (1971). Lee has recently written two verse collections—*Earthquakes and Sun Rise Missions: Poetry and Essays of Black Renewal 1973–1983* (1984) and *Killing Memory, Seeking Ancestors* (1987)—and, more recently, two works of nonfiction: *Black Men: Obsolete, Single, Dangerous? (The Afrikan American Family in Transition)* (1990) and *Claiming Earth: Race, Rage, Rape, Redemption: Blacks Seeking a Culture of Enlightened Empowerment* (1994). He is president of the African American Publishers', Booksellers' and Writers' Association and teaches at Chicago State University.

RICHARD A. LONG (1927–) was known for his scholarship and his standing in the academic community long before his poetry appeared. His impressive two-volume collection, *Afro-American Writing*, edited in collaboration with Eugenia W. Collier, became available from New York University Press in 1972. He is associated with Atlanta University and has been a lecturer at Harvard and elsewhere. *Ascending: Poems* was published in 1975, followed by two books on African American culture and dance. He is Atticus Hayward Professor of Interdisciplinary Studies at Emory University.

AUDRE LORDE (1934–92) was a New Yorker born and bred, as rural folks might say. She taught at the City Colleges of New York and served as poet-in-residence at Tougaloo College in Mississippi under a National Endowment for the Arts grant. Her first collection of poems was *The First Cities* (1968). A second volume, *Cables to Rage* (1970), was published in London. Lorde described herself as a "black lesbian feminist mother lover poet." She expressed anger toward racial oppression, urban blight, and personal misfortune, but her poetry was infused with hope and spiritual enlightenment. Between 1973 and 1988 she published seven more poetry collections, including *From a Land Where People Live*, which was nominated for the National Book Award for Poetry; the novel *Zami: A New Spelling of My Name*; and *Sister Outsider: Essays and Speeches*.

CLAUDE MCKAY (1891–1948) was first published in his native Jamaica, British West Indies. In his early twenties, however, he came to the United States to study agriculture at Tuskegee Institute in Alabama and then at Kansas State University. After two years, he moved to New York City, where he was drawn into the literary life. He went to Europe for the first time in 1919, spent a year in London, and published there a slight volume of poems, called *Spring in New Hampshire* (1920). Back in the United States again, he became associate editor of the *Liberator* under Max Eastman. *Harlem Shadows* (1922) was his next collection of poems. For the rest of his life McKay published only prose, but off and on he wrote poetry, and some of his later pieces are included in the posthumously published *Selected Poems* (1953).

NAOMI LONG MADGETT (1923–   ) was born in Norfolk, Virginia, but grew up in East Orange, New Jersey, and St. Louis, Missouri. Since 1956 she has lived in Detroit, where she was a high-school teacher for thirteen years. In 1965 she was the first recipient of the Mott Fellowship in English at Oakland University. Thereafter, she taught at Eastern Michigan University in Ypsilanti, where she was Professor of English. She is the author of four volumes of poetry, among them *Star by Star* (1965, rev. 1970) and *Pink Ladies in the Afternoon* (1972). Her poems have appeared in more than fifty anthologies and a number of journals in this country and abroad, and her papers are stored in the Special Collections of the Fisk University Library. She is a graduate of Virginia State College and Wayne State University. Since 1974, Naomi Long Madgett has served as publisher and editor of Lotus Press, and since 1984, as Professor Emerita of Eastern Michigan University. Two additional poetry collections are *Exits and Entrances* (1978) and *Octavia and Other Poems* (1988).

CLARENCE MAJOR (1936–   ) was born in Atlanta, Georgia, but grew up and attended school in Chicago. His poems have been published in *Black Orpheus* and other small magazines, for which he has also written about painting. Occasionally he contributes short stories. He now lives and teaches creative writing in New York City. Author of the novel *The All-Night Visitors*, he has also published several collections of poems, such as *Swallow the Lake* (1970) and *Symptoms and Madness* (1971) and has appeared in many anthologies, including *Black Voices*, *In the Time of Revolution*, *The Writing on the Wall*, and *Where Is Vietnam?* He served two terms as writer-in-residence at the Pennsylvania Advancement School. Between 1971 and 1989 he wrote eight books of poetry and the novels *All-Night Visitors*, *No*, *Bone Structure*, and *Emergency Exit*, which are considered important experimental works of contemporary fiction.

PAULI MURRAY (1910–85) wrote a family history, *Proud Shoes*, which was published in 1956. Like Samuel Allen and Bruce McM. Wright, she was an occasional poet and a practicing lawyer. Born in Baltimore, Maryland, Miss Murray began her education in North Carolina and continued it in New York and California, among other places. Her poetry appeared in *Common Ground*, *South Today*, and *Saturday Review of Literature*. *Dark Testament and Other Poems* was published in 1970. Murray received law degrees from Howard, Yale, and the University of California at Berkeley, and taught law throughout America and Africa. In 1974 she became the first black woman to be ordained as an Episcopal priest.

LARRY NEAL (1937–81) was born in Atlanta, Georgia, and reared in Philadelphia. He earned a degree from Lincoln University in Pennsylvania and was a graduate student at the University of Pennsylvania. He served on the staff of magazines such as *Liberator* and *The Cricket* and contributed to *Journal of Black Poetry*. He edited *Black Fire* (1968) with LeRoi Jones. Neal taught English at New York University, Wesleyan, and Yale universities, and in 1976–79 was both Executive Director of the Commission on the Arts and Humanities in Washington, D.C., and Andrew W. Mellon Humanist in Residence at Howard University. Between 1976 and 1978 he was also education director of the Panther Party. Neal's later poetry volumes are *Black Boogaloo: Notes on Black Liberation* (1969) and *Hoodoo Hollerin' Bebop Ghosts* (1971).

EFFIE LEE NEWSOME (1885–1979) lived for most of her life in Wilberforce, Ohio. Her book *Gladiola Garden* (1940), a collection of poems for children, is mainly concerned with nature. She edited the children's column in the periodicals *Crisis* and *Opportunity*, where her poems also appeared.

GLORIA C. ODEN (1923–   ) was a member of the staff of *The Urbanite: Images of the American Negro. The Naked Frame: A Love Poem and Sonnets* (1952) won for her a John Hay Whitney Opportunity Fellowship for creative writing. Her college was Howard University in Washington, D.C. She taught in the English Department of the University of Maryland in Baltimore.

MYRON O'HIGGINS (1918–   ), born in Chicago, belongs to the tribe of wandering poets. At Howard University in Washington, D.C., he came under the influence and guidance of Sterling A. Brown, but his writing earned him Lucy Moten and Julius Rosenwald fellowships, the army took him abroad, and so his travels began. His poems have been published in magazines and anthologies and in *The Lion and the Archer* (1948), which he and Robert Hayden put out privately in a limited edition.

FRANK LAMONT PHILLIPS (1953–   ) was born in Elroy, Arizona, and was graduated from Fisk University. He submitted poetry to contests while in high school and was awarded honorable mention in the *Scholastic Magazine* contest and a merit award in the *Atlantic Monthly* Creative Writing Contest for 1971.

OLIVER PITCHER (1923–   ) is a playwright, poet, director, and teacher. Born in Massachusetts and educated at Bard College, the Dramatic Workshop of the New School, and the American Negro Theater, he has had works published both here and abroad. His play *The One* was presented by The Negro Ensemble Company in New York and was published in *Black Drama Anthology*. Two other plays, *Shampoo* and *Crap Game*, became Off-Broadway productions. A booklet of poems, *Dust of Silence*, was published in 1958. Mr. Pitcher taught black theater at Vassar College and served as poet-in-residence at Atlanta University Center, where he taught poetry and creative writing. He also taught at Emory University.

DUDLEY RANDALL (1914–   ) is the poet-founder of Broadside Press in Detroit, Michigan. A former librarian and teacher, he revived the old custom of printing single poems on broadsides at a few cents each. The success of this avocation led to expansion of the operation. In 1966 he visited Paris, Prague, and the Soviet Union, with a delegation of black artists. That same year, he received the Wayne State University Tomkins Award for Poetry. He was poet-in-residence at the University of Detroit. His works include *Love You* and *More to Remember*, both published in 1971, and *Black Poetry: A Supplement to Anthologies Which Exclude Black Poets*. He wrote *A Litany of Friends: New and Selected Poems* (1981) and *Homage and Hoyt Fuller* (1984).

CONRAD KENT RIVERS (1933–68) was born in Atlantic City, New Jersey. His poems were published in the *Antioch* and *Kenyon Reviews*, and a booklet of his poems appeared in 1959 under the title *Perchance to Dream, Othello. These Black Bodies and This Sunburnt Face* was published in Cleveland in 1962. Breman brought out his fourth volume of poetry, entitled *The Still Voice of Harlem*, and in 1971 Broadside published his *Wright Poems–Essay by Ronald Fair*.

ANNE SPENCER (1882–1975) lived for most of her life in Lynchburg, Virginia, where she was for years the librarian of the Dunbar High School. Tending her garden was her long-time interest. In 1970, the Friendship Press published her *African Panorama*.

MELVIN B. TOLSON (1898–1966) was an English teacher at Wiley College in Marshall, Texas, and at Langston University in Oklahoma after he was graduated from Lincoln University in Pennsylvania and Columbia University in New York. He was a debating coach, worked with drama clubs, and gave many public readings of his poetry. His "Dark Symphony" appeared in *The Atlantic Monthly* after winning a poetry prize in Chicago and was included in his book *Rendezvous with America* (1944). His *Libretto for the Republic of Liberia* was published in 1953 with an introduction by Allen Tate. His *Harlem Gallery* (1965) was introduced by Karl Shapiro.

JEAN TOOMER'S (1893–1967) poems, sketches, short stories, and plays of Negro life appeared in the early 1920s. They received praise from Sherwood Anderson, Hart Crane, Gorham Munson, John McClure, and many others, and his book *Cane*, in which they were collected in 1923, was introduced enthusiastically by Waldo Frank. About ten years later, Toomer "disappeared," so far as most of his former literary associates were concerned. In the 1970s, his papers, his correspondence, his unpublished manuscripts, the record of his exile, if that is the word, were found. In any case, Toomer was born in Washington, D.C., the grandson of P.B.S. Pinchback, the Negro who served for a short time as acting governor of Louisiana and was then elected to the United States Senate but denied his seat.

JAMES VAUGHN (1929–   ) was born and educated in Xenia, Ohio. After serving in the army, he earned two degrees at Ohio State University and was for a time an English teacher at Southern University in Louisiana and at West Virginia State College. From 1966 to 1970 he taught at the University of Riyadh, Saudi Arabia, and since the fall of 1971 he has taught at the Herbert H. Lehman College of the City University of New York.

MARGARET WALKER (1915–   ) wrote a collection of poems which was accepted by the State University of Iowa in place of the usual Master of Arts dissertation, and she was awarded the degree in 1940. She taught English at Jackson College, Jackson, Mississippi; Livingston College, Salisbury, North Carolina; and West Virginia State College. She was born in Birmingham, Alabama, the daughter of a minister, and has herself reared a large family. Her first novel, *Jubilee* (1966), was awarded a Houghton Mifflin Literary Prize and became a ringing success in a paperback edition. She holds a Ph.D. from the University of Iowa. Her work has been included in *Black Voices* (1968), and her collections are entitled *For My People* (1968), *Prophets for a New Day* (1970), *October Journey* (1973), and *This Is My Century: New and Collected Poems* (1988).

CHARLES ENOCH WHEELER (1909–   ) was born in Augusta, Georgia, but later attended school in New York.

BRUCE MCM. WRIGHT (1918–83) was graduated from Lincoln University in Pennsylvania in 1942 and then served in the First Infantry Division in Europe during World War II, where he was wounded twice and received several decorations. He was trained for the law at Fordham University and Yale University Law School; at Yale he was quondam Chief Justice of the Yale Law School Moot Court of Appeals. In the 1970s, he was a judge in the Criminal Court of the City of New York. While he was still in the army, Wright's poems, *From the Proud Tower* (1944), were published in Wales. Thereafter, his poetry was featured in French, Swedish, Slavic, as well as English anthologies.

RICHARD WRIGHT's (1908–60) autobiography, *Black Boy*, was a sensational Book-of-the-Month selection in 1945. Five years earlier, his hard-fisted novel, *Native Son*, had a similar impact. Since his death in 1960, the meteoric career of this Mississippi-born writer has frequently been recalled, and some previously unpublished poetry has come to light. After the struggles detailed in the autobiography, Wright lived and wrote in New York for a while, traveled extensively, but spent most of his later years with his family in Paris.

MARVIN WYCHE, JR. (1951–   ), described himself at one time as "a twenty-one-year-old blood from Englewood, New Jersey." He went on to say: "As a first-year poet, I've attempted to reproduce personal experience in hopes of reaching as large a section of black and oppressed people as those experiences will allow. As a second-year poet, I will do the same." He attracted attention as a college junior by winning a national poetry contest sponsored by the United Negro College Fund in association with *Reader's Digest* (1972).

FRANK YERBY (1916–91) was noted for his brightly colored historical romances, but his

227

writing career began with poetry and short stories in the *Fisk Herald* when he was a student, about the time of Samuel Allen, Yvonne Gregory, and their group. The true Yerby fan, of which there are many indeed, should be able to relate the poetry to the prose without difficulty. Among his later books were *Judas, My Brother* (1968), *Speak Now* (1969), *Dahomean* (1971), *Vixens* (1972), *The Girl from Storyville* (1972), *Flood Tide* (1972), and *Golden Hawk* (1972). Yerby was born in Augusta, Georgia, but beginning in the 1950s made his home in Spain.

Index of Titles

230

Acknowledgments

FOR PERMISSION to reprint the poems in this book thanks are due Frank Yerby, Mrs. Ellen Wright, Robert Hayden, the other poets and copyright holders whose works are represented, and the following publishers:

Bookman Associates—for "The Tropics in New York," "Outcast," "St. Isaac's Church, Petrograd," "Flame-Heart," "If We Must Die," and "The White House" from *The Selected Poems of Claude McKay*.

Corinth Books and Totem Press—for selections from *Preface to a Twenty Volume Suicide Note*, by LeRoi Jones, © 1961, LeRoi Jones.

Coward-McCann—for "Rhapsody" and "Scintilla" from *Selected Poems* by William Stanley Braithwaite, © 1948 by William Stanley Braithwaite.

Dodd, Mead & Co.—for "Dark Symphony" from *Rendezvous with Death* by Melvin B. Tolson, copyright 1944 by Dodd, Mead & Co.; for "Dawn," "Compensation," "The Debt," "Life," "My Sort o' Man," "The Party," "A Song," "Sympathy," and "We Wear the Mask" from *The Complete Poems of Paul Laurence Dunbar*.

Farrar, Straus & Cudahy—for "Sorrow Is the Only Faithful One" and "Drunken Lover" from *Powerful Long Ladder* by Owen Dodson.

Harcourt, Brace & Co.—for "Sister Lou" and "When de Saints Go Ma'chin' Home" by Sterling A. Brown.

Harper & Row—for "Heritage," "Yet Do I Marvel," "Four Epitaphs," and "Simon the Cyrenian Speaks" from *Color* by Countee Cullen, copyright 1925 by Harper & Row, Publishers, Inc., and "That Bright Chimeric Beast" from *The Black Christ and Other Poems* by Countee Cullen, copyright 1929 by Harper & Row, Publishers, Inc.; for "Flags," "The Old-Marrieds," and "Piano After War" from *A Street in Bronzeville* by Gwendolyn Brooks, copyright 1944, 1945 by Gwendolyn Brooks Blakely, and "The Chicago *Defender* Sends a Man to Little Rock" from *The Bean Eaters* by Gwendolyn Brooks, copyright © 1960 by Gwendolyn Brooks.

Alfred A. Knopf—for the following poems by Langston Hughes: "Cross," "Jazzonia," "The Negro Speaks of Rivers," "I, Too," "Dream Variations," and "Mother to Son," all copyright, 1926 by Alfred A. Knopf, Inc., renewed, 1954 by Langston Hughes; and "Bound No'th Blues," copyright, 1932 by Alfred A. Knopf, Inc., renewed 1960 by Langston Hughes, and "Personal," copyright 1947 by Langston Hughes.

Liveright Publishing Corp.—for "Song of the Son" and "Georgia Dusk" from *Cane* by Jean Toomer, copyright © R-1951 by Jean Toomer.

The Viking Press—for "O Black and Unknown Bards" from *Saint Peter Relates an Incident* by James Weldon Johnson, copyright 1917, 1935 by James Weldon Johnson, 1962 by Grace Nail Johnson, and "Go Down Death" from *God's Trombones* by James Weldon Johnson, copyright 1927 by The Viking Press, Inc., 1954 by Grace Nail Johnson.

Yale University Press—for "For My People" and "Molly Means" from *For My People* by Margaret Walker.

Thanks are also due Langston Hughes for "Brass Spittoons," "Lenox Avenue Mural," "Pennsylvania Station," "I Dream a World," and "Without Benefit of Declaration," and Owen Dodson for "Sickle Pears," "Hymn Written After Jeremiah Preached to Me in a Dream," "Yardbird's Skull," and "Sailors on Leave."

Special acknowledgment is given to the following poets and publishers for the poems added to the revised edition:

Lucille Clifton, "Good Times," from *Good Times,* by Lucille Clifton, © 1969 by Lucille Clifton. Reprinted by permission of Random House, Inc.

Nikki Giovanni, "My Poem," "Nikki-Rosa," "Knoxville, Tennessee," and "The Funeral of Martin Luther King, Jr.," from *Black Judgement,* © by Nikki Giovanni. "Kidnap Poem" and "A Robin's Poem," from *Re: Creation,* © 1968 by Nikki Giovanni. Reprinted by permission of Broadside Press, Detroit, Michigan.

Calvin C. Hernton, "Young Negro Poet," © 1962 by Calvin C. Hernton and reprinted by permission of the author.

Helen Armstead Johnson, "Affirmation," © 1966 by Joseph Leonard Grucci and reprinted by permission of Joseph L. Grucci, editor of *Pivot.* "Philodendron," © 1967 by Joseph L. Grucci and reprinted by his permission.

Bob Kaufman, "I Have Folded My Sorrows," "African Dream," "Battle Report," "Forget to Not," from Bob Kaufman, *Solitudes Crowded with Loneliness,* © 1965 by Bob Kaufman. Reprinted by permission of New Directions Publishing Corporation. "Cocoa Morning," © 1967 by Bob Kaufman. Reprinted by permission of City Lights Books.

Don L. Lee, "But He Was Cool," "Assassination," from *Don't Cry, Scream,* © 1969 by Don L. Lee. "Education," "Stereo," from *Think Black,* © 1967 by Don L. Lee. Reprinted by permission of Broadside Press, Detroit, Michigan.

Richard A. Long, "Hearing James Brown at the Café des Nattes," © September 1971 by *Black World.* Reprinted by permission of *Black World* and Richard A. Long. "Juan de Pareja," reprinted by permission of the author.

Audre Lorde, "If You Come Softly," © 1968 by Audre Lorde. Reprinted by permission of the author.

Naomi Long Madgett, "Woman with Flower," from *Star by Star* © 1965, 1970 by Naomi Long Madgett. Reprinted by permission of the author.

Larry Neal, "Malcolm X—An Autobiography," from *Black Boogaloo,* © 1968 by Larry Neal. Reprinted by permission of the author.

Frank Lamont Phillips, "No Smiles," "Genealogy," "Maryuma," reprinted by permission of the author.

Marvin Wyche, Jr., "Five Sense," © 1972 by Marvin Wyche, Jr. Reprinted by permission of the author. "And She Was Bad," "We Rainclouds," and "Leslie," reprinted by permission of the author.